Collins

Collins
Spanish
Words

HarperCollins Publishers
Westerhill Road
Bishopbriggs
Glasgow
G64 2QT
Great Britain

First Edition 2006

© HarperCollins Publishers 2006

ISBN-13   978-0-00-723156-0
ISBN-10   0-00-723156-3

Collins® and Bank of English® are registered
trademarks of HarperCollins Publishers
Limited

www.collins.co.uk

A catalogue record for this book is available
from the British Library

Typeset by Davidson Pre-Press, Glasgow

Printed in Italy by Rotolito Lombarda SpA

Acknowledgements
We would like to thank those authors and
publishers who kindly gave permission for
copyright material to be used in the Collins
Word Web. We would also like to thank
Times Newspapers Ltd for providing
valuable data.

PUBLISHING DIRECTOR
Lorna Knight

EDITORIAL DIRECTOR
Michela Clari

MANAGING EDITOR
Maree Airlie

PROJECT CO-ORDINATOR
Gaëlle Amiot-Cadey

CONTRIBUTORS
José Martín Galera
Val McNulty
Julie Muleba
Victoria Romero Cerro

William Collins' dream of knowledge for all began with the publication of his first book in 1819. A self-educated mill worker, he not only enriched millions of lives, but also founded a flourishing publishing house. Today, staying true to this spirit, Collins books are packed with inspiration, innovation, and practical expertise. They place you at the centre of a world of possibility and give you exactly what you need to explore it.

Language is the key to this exploration, and at the heart of Collins Dictionaries is language as it is really used. New words, phrases, and meanings spring up every day, and all of them are captured and analysed by the Collins Word Web. Constantly updated, and with over 2.5 billion entries, this living language resource is unique to our dictionaries.

Words are tools for life. And a Collins Dictionary makes them work for you.

Collins. Do more.

contents

6 contents

Collins Easy Learning Spanish Words is designed for both young and adult learners. Whether you are starting to learn Spanish for the first time, revising for school exams or simply want to brush up on your Spanish, *Collins Easy Learning Spanish Words* offers you the information you require in a clear and accessible format.

This book is divided into 50 topics, arranged in alphabetical order. This thematic approach enables you to learn related words and phrases together, so that you can become confident in using particular vocabulary in context.

Vocabulary within each topic is divided into nouns and useful phrases which are aimed at helping you to express yourself in idiomatic Spanish. Vocabulary within each topic is graded to help you prioritize your learning. Essential words include the basic words you will need to be able to communicate effectively, important words help expand your knowledge, and useful words provide additional vocabulary which will enable you to express yourself more fully.

Nouns are grouped by gender: masculine ("el") nouns are given on the left-hand page, and feminine ("la") nouns on the right-hand page, enabling you to memorize words according to their gender. In addition, all feminine forms of adjectives are shown, as are irregular plurals.

At the end of the book you will find a list of supplementary vocabulary, grouped according to part of speech – adjective, verb, noun and so on. This is vocabulary which you will come across in many everyday situations.

Finally, there is an English index which lists all the essential and important nouns given under the topic headings for quick reference.

Collins Easy Learning Spanish Words helps you to consolidate your language learning. Together with the other titles in the *Easy Learning* range you can be sure that you have all the help you need when learning Spanish at your fingertips.

ABBREVIATIONS

adj	adjective
adv	adverb
algn	alguien
conj	conjunction
f	feminine
inv	invariable
LAm	word used in Latin America
m	masculine
m+f	masculine and feminine form
Mex	word used in Mexico
n	noun
pl	plural
prep	preposition
sb	somebody
sing	singular
Sp	word used in Spain
sth	something

The swung dash ~ is used to indicate the basic elements of the compound and appropriate endings are then added.

PLURALS AND GENDER

In Spanish, if a noun ends in a vowel it generally takes –s in the plural (casa > casas). If it ends in a consonant (including y) it generally takes –es in the plural (reloj > relojes). If it doesn't follow these rules, then the plural will be given in the text.

Although most masculine nouns take "el" and most feminine nouns take "la", you will find a few nouns grouped under feminine words which take "el" (el agua water; el arca chest; el aula classroom) because they are actually feminine.

ESSENTIAL WORDS (*masculine*)

el	**aeropuerto**	airport
el	**agente de viajes**	travel agent
el	**alquiler de coches**	car hire
el	**avión** (*pl* aviones)	plane
el	**billete** (*Sp*), el **boleto** (*LAm*)	ticket
el	**bolso**	bag
el	**carnet** (*or* carné) **de identidad**	ID card
	(*pl* carnets *or* carnés ~ ~)	
el	**enlace**	connection
el	**equipaje**	luggage
el	**equipaje de mano**	hand luggage
el	**horario**	timetable
el	**número**	number
el	**oficial de aduanas**	customs officer
el	**pasajero**	passenger
el	**pasaporte**	passport
el	**(precio del) billete** (*Sp*) *or* **boleto** (*LAm*)	fare
el	**retraso**	delay
los	**servicios**	toilets
el	**taxi**	taxi
el	**turista**	tourist
el	**viaje**	trip
el	**viajero**	traveller

USEFUL PHRASES

viajar en avión to travel by plane

un billete (*Sp*) *or* boleto (*LAm*) de ida a single ticket

un billete (*Sp*) *or* boleto (*LAm*) de ida y vuelta, un boleto redondo (*Mex*)
a return ticket

reservar un billete (*Sp*) *or* boleto (*LAm*) de avión to book a plane ticket

"por avión" "by airmail"

facturar el equipaje to check in one's luggage

perdí el enlace I missed my connection

el avión ha despegado/ha aterrizado the plane has taken off/has landed

el panel de llegadas/salidas the arrivals/departures board

el vuelo número 776 procedente de Madrid/con destino Madrid flight
number 776 from Madrid/to Madrid

ESSENTIAL WORDS *(feminine)*

la	aduana	customs
la	agente de viajes	travel agent
la	cancelación *(pl* cancelaciones)	cancellation
la	duty free	duty-free (shop)
la	entrada	entrance
la	información *(pl* informaciones)	information desk; information
la	llegada	arrival
la	maleta	bag; suitcase
la	oficial de aduanas	customs officer
la	pasajera	passenger
la	puerta de embarque	departure gate
la	reserva	reservation
la	salida	departure; exit
la	salida de emergencia	emergency exit
la	tarifa	fare
la	tarjeta de embarque	boarding card
la	turista	tourist
la	viajera	traveller

USEFUL PHRASES

recoger el equipaje to collect one's luggage
"recogida de equipajes" "baggage reclaim"
pasar por la aduana to go through customs
tengo algo que declarar I have something to declare
no tengo nada que declarar I have nothing to declare
registrar el equipaje to search the luggage

IMPORTANT WORDS (*masculine*)

el	accidente de avión	plane crash
el	billete electrónico	e-ticket
el	carrito	trolley
el	cinturón de seguridad	seat belt
	(*pl* cinturones ~~)	
el	helicóptero	helicopter
el	mapa	map
el	mareo (en avión)	airsickness
el	piloto	pilot
el	reloj	clock
el	vuelo	flight

USEFUL WORDS (*masculine*)

el	asiento	seat
el	aterrizaje	landing
el	auxiliar de vuelo	steward; flight attendant
el	cambiador para bebés	mother and baby room
el	control de seguridad	security check
el	controlador aéreo	air-traffic controller
los	derechos de aduana	customs duty
el	despegue	take-off
el	detector de metales	metal detector
el	embarque	boarding
el	horario	timetable
el	jumbo	jumbo jet
los	mandos	controls
el	paracaídas (*pl inv*)	parachute
el	radar	radar
el	reactor	jet plane/engine
el	satélite	satellite terminal
el	veraneante	holiday-maker

USEFUL PHRASES

a bordo on board; "prohibido fumar" "no smoking"
"abróchense el cinturón de seguridad" "fasten your seat belts"
estamos sobrevolando Londres we are flying over London
me estoy mareando I am feeling sick; secuestrar un avión to hijack a plane

IMPORTANT WORDS *(feminine)*

la	**duración** *(pl* duraciones)	length; duration
la	**escalera mecánica**	escalator
la	**piloto**	pilot
la	**sala de embarque**	departure lounge
la	**velocidad**	speed

USEFUL WORDS *(feminine)*

el	**ala** *(pl f* las alas)	wing
la	**altitud**	altitude
la	**altura**	height
la	**auxiliar de vuelo**	air hostess; flight attendant
la	**barrera del sonido**	sound barrier
la	**bolsa de aire**	air pocket
la	**caja negra**	black box
la	**cinta transportadora**	carousel
la	**controladora aérea**	air-traffic controller
la	**escala**	stopover
la	**etiqueta**	label
la	**hélice**	propeller
la	**línea aérea**	airline
la	**pista (de aterrizaje)**	runway
la	**terminal**	terminal
la	**tienda libre de impuestos**	duty-free shop
la	**torre de control**	control tower
la	**tripulación** *(pl* tripulaciones)	crew
la	**turbulencia**	turbulence
la	**ventanilla**	window
la	**veraneante**	holiday-maker

USEFUL PHRASES

"pasajeros del vuelo AB251 con destino Madrid embarquen por la puerta 51"
  "flight AB251 to Madrid now boarding at gate 51"
hicimos escala en Nueva York **we stopped over in New York**
un aterrizaje forzoso *or* de emergencia **an emergency landing**
un aterrizaje violento **a crash landing**
cigarrillos libres de impuestos **duty-free cigarettes**

ESSENTIAL WORDS *(masculine)*

el	animal	animal
el	buey *(pl ~es)*	ox
el	caballo	horse
el	cerdo	pig
el	conejo	rabbit
el	cordero	lamb
el	elefante	elephant
el	gato	cat
el	gatito	kitten
el	hámster *(pl ~s)*	hamster
el	león *(pl leones)*	lion
el	pájaro	bird
el	perro	dog
el	perrito	puppy
el	cachorro	puppy
el	pelaje	fur, coat
el	pelo	coat, hair
el	pescado	fish
el	pez *(pl peces)*	fish
el	potro	foal
el	ratón *(pl ratones)*	mouse
el	ternero	calf
el	tigre	tiger
el	zoo *(pl ~s)*	zoo
el	zoológico	zoo

USEFUL PHRASES

me gustan los gatos, odio las serpientes, prefiero los ratones **I like cats, I hate snakes, I prefer mice**

tenemos 12 animales en casa **we have 12 pets in our house**

no tenemos animales en casa **we have no pets in our house**

los animales salvajes **wild animals**

los animales domésticos *or* las mascotas **pets**

el ganado **livestock**

meter un animal en una jaula **to put an animal in a cage**

liberar un animal **to set an animal free**

ESSENTIAL WORDS *(feminine)*

el	**ave** *(pl f* las aves)	bird
la	**gata**	cat *(female)*
la	**oveja**	ewe
la	**perra**	dog *(female)*
la	**tortuga**	tortoise
la	**vaca**	cow

IMPORTANT WORDS *(feminine)*

la	**cola**	tail
la	**jaula**	cage

USEFUL PHRASES

el perro ladra **the dog barks;** gruñe **it growls**

el gato maulla **the cat miaows;** ronronea **it purrs**

me gusta la equitación *or* montar a caballo **I like horse-riding**

a caballo **on horseback**

"cuidado con el perro" **"beware of the dog"**

"no se admiten perros" **"no dogs allowed"**

"¡quieto!" *(to dog)* **"down!"**

los derechos de los animales **animal rights**

USEFUL WORDS *(masculine)*

el	asno	donkey
el	burro	donkey
el	camello	camel
el	canguro	kangaroo
el	caparazón *(pl* caparazones)	shell *(of tortoise)*
el	casco	hoof
el	cerdo	pig
el	ciervo	stag
el	cocodrilo	crocodile
el	colmillo	tusk
el	conejillo de Indias	guinea pig
el	cuerno	horn
el	erizo	hedgehog
el	hipopótamo	hippopotamus
el	hocico	snout
el	lobo	wolf
el	macho cabrío	billy goat
el	mono	monkey
el	mulo	mule
el	murciélago	bat
el	oso	bear
el	oso polar	polar bear
el	pavo	turkey
el	pony *(pl* ~s)	pony
el	rinoceronte	rhinoceros
el	sapo	toad
el	tiburón *(pl* tiburones)	shark
el	topo	mole
el	toro	bull
el	zorro	fox

USEFUL WORDS (feminine)

la	ardilla	squirrel
el	asta (pl f las astas)	antler
la	ballena	whale
la	boca	mouth
la	bolsa	pouch (of kangaroo)
la	cabra	(nanny) goat
la	crin	mane
la	culebra	(grass) snake
la	foca	seal
la	garra	claw
la	jirafa	giraffe
la	joroba	hump (of camel)
la	leona	lioness
la	liebre	hare
la	melena	mane
la	mula	mule
la	pajarería	pet shop
la	pata	paw
la	pezuña	hoof
la	piel	fur; hide (of cow, elephant etc)
la	rana	frog
las	rayas	stripes (of zebra)
la	serpiente	snake
la	tienda de animales	pet shop
la	tigresa	tigress
la	trampa	trap
la	trompa	trunk (of elephant)
la	yegua	mare
la	zebra	zebra

ESSENTIAL WORDS (masculine)

el	casco	helmet
el	ciclismo	cycling
el	ciclista	cyclist
el	faro	lamp
el	freno	brake
el	neumático	tyre

IMPORTANT WORDS (masculine)

el	pinchazo	puncture

USEFUL WORDS (masculine)

el	ascenso	climb
el	candado	padlock
el	carril bici	cycle lane
el	descarrilamiento	derailleur
el	descenso	descent
el	eje	hub
el	guardabarros (pl inv) (Sp)	mudguard
el	kit de reparación de pinchazos (pl ~s ~~~~)	puncture repair kit
el	manillar	handlebars
el	pedal	pedal
el	portaequipajes (pl inv)	carrier
el	radio	spoke
el	reflector	reflector
el	sillín (pl sillines)	saddle
el	timbre	bell

USEFUL PHRASES

ir en bici(cleta) to go by bike, to cycle
vine en bici(cleta) I came by bike
viajar to travel
a toda velocidad at full speed
cambiar de marchas to change gears
pararse to stop
frenar bruscamente to brake suddenly

ESSENTIAL WORDS (feminine)

la	**bici**	bike
la	**bicicleta**	bicycle
la	**bicicleta de montaña**	mountain bike
la	**vuelta ciclista a España**	Tour of Spain

IMPORTANT WORDS (feminine)

la	**rueda**	wheel
la	**velocidad**	speed; gear

USEFUL WORDS (feminine)

la	**alforja**	pannier
la	**barra**	crossbar
la	**bomba**	pump
la	**cadena**	chain
la	**cuesta**	slope
la	**cumbre**	top (of hill)
la	**dínamo**	dynamo
la	**luz delantera** (pl luces ~s)	front light
la	**pendiente**	slope
la	**salpicadera** (Mex)	mudguard
la	**subida**	climb
la	**válvula**	valve

USEFUL PHRASES

dar una vuelta or pasear en bici(cleta) to go for a bike ride
tener un pinchazo or una rueda pinchada to have a puncture
arreglar un pinchazo to mend a puncture
la rueda delantera/trasera the front/back wheel
inflar las ruedas to blow up the tyres
brillante, reluciente shiny
oxidado(a) rusty
fluorescente fluorescent

ESSENTIAL WORDS (*masculine*)

el	cielo	sky
el	gallo	cock
el	ganso	goose
el	loro	parrot
el	pájaro	bird
el	pato	duck
el	pavo	turkey
el	periquito	budgie

USEFUL WORDS (*masculine*)

el	avestruz (*pl* avestruces)	ostrich
el	búho	owl
el	buitre	vulture
el	canario	canary
el	chochín (*pl* chochines)	wren
el	cisne	swan
el	cuervo	raven; crow
el	cuco	cuckoo
el	estornino	starling
el	faisán (*pl* faisanes)	pheasant
el	gorrión (*pl* gorriones)	sparrow
el	halcón (*pl* halcones)	falcon
el	herrerillo	bluetit
el	huevo	egg
el	martín pescador (*pl* martines ~es)	kingfisher
el	mirlo	blackbird
el	nido	nest
el	pájaro carpintero	woodpecker
el	pavo real	peacock
el	petirrojo	robin
el	pico	beak
el	pingüino	penguin
el	ruiseñor	nightingale
el	tordo	thrush
el	urogallo	grouse

ESSENTIAL WORDS *(feminine)*

la **gallina**	hen

USEFUL WORDS *(feminine)*

el **águila** (*pl f* las águilas)	eagle
el **ala** (*pl f* las alas)	wing
la **alondra**	lark
el **ave** (*pl f* las aves)	bird
el **ave de rapiña** (*pl f* las ~s ~~)	bird of prey
el **ave rapaz** (*pl f* las ~s rapaces)	bird of prey
la **cigüeña**	stork
la **codorniz** (*pl* codornices)	quail
la **gaviota**	seagull
la **golondrina**	swallow
la **grajilla**	jackdaw
la **jaula**	cage
la **paloma**	pigeon; dove
la **perdiz** (*pl* perdices)	partridge
la **pluma**	feather
la **urraca**	magpie

USEFUL PHRASES

volar to fly
emprender vuelo to fly away
construir un nido to build a nest
silbar to whistle
cantar to sing
la gente los mete en jaulas people put them in cages
hibernar to hibernate
poner un huevo to lay an egg
un ave migratoria a migratory bird

ESSENTIAL WORDS *(masculine)*

el	**brazo**	arm
el	**cabello**	hair
el	**corazón** *(pl* corazones)	heart
el	**cuerpo**	body
el	**dedo**	finger
el	**diente**	tooth
el	**estómago**	stomach
el	**ojo**	eye
el	**pelo**	hair
el	**pie**	foot
el	**rostro**	face

IMPORTANT WORDS *(masculine)*

el	**cuello**	neck
el	**hombro**	shoulder
el	**pecho**	chest; bust
el	**pulgar**	thumb
el	**tobillo**	ankle

USEFUL PHRASES
de pie standing
sentado(a) sitting
tumbado(a) lying

ESSENTIAL WORDS *(feminine)*

la	**boca**	mouth
la	**cabeza**	head
la	**espalda**	back
la	**garganta**	throat
la	**mano**	hand
la	**nariz** *(pl* narices)	nose
la	**oreja**	ear
la	**pierna**	leg
la	**rodilla**	knee

IMPORTANT WORDS *(feminine)*

la	**barbilla**	chin
la	**cara**	face
la	**ceja**	eyebrow
la	**frente**	forehead
la	**lengua**	tongue
la	**mejilla**	cheek
la	**piel**	skin
la	**sangre**	blood
la	**voz** *(pl* voces)	voice

USEFUL PHRASES

grande big
alto(a) tall
pequeño(a) small
bajo(a) short
gordo(a) fat
flaco(a) skinny
delgado(a) slim
bonito(a) pretty
feo(a) ugly

USEFUL WORDS *(masculine)*

el	**cerebro**	brain
el	**codo**	elbow
el	**cutis** *(pl inv)*	skin, complexion
el	**dedo del pie**	toe
el	**dedo índice**	forefinger
el	**dedo gordo**	the big toe
los	**dedos del pie**	toes
el	**esqueleto**	skeleton
el	**gesto**	gesture
el	**hígado**	liver
el	**hueso**	bone
el	**labio**	lip
el	**músculo**	muscle
el	**muslo**	thigh
el	**párpado**	eyelid
el	**pulmón** *(pl* pulmones)	lung
el	**puño**	fist
el	**rasgo**	feature
el	**riñón** *(pl* riñones)	kidney
el	**seno**	breast
el	**talle**	waist
el	**talón** *(pl* talones)	heel
el	**trasero**	bottom

USEFUL PHRASES

sonarse (la nariz) to blow one's nose
cortarse las uñas to cut one's nails
cortarse el pelo to have one's hair cut
encogerse de hombros to shrug one's shoulders
asentir/decir que sí con la cabeza to nod one's head
negar/decir que no con la cabeza to shake one's head
ver to see; oír to hear; sentir to feel
oler to smell; tocar to touch; probar to taste
estrechar la mano a alguien to shake hands with somebody
saludar a alguien con la mano to wave at somebody
señalar algo to point at something

USEFUL WORDS *(feminine)*

la	**arteria**	artery
la	**cadera**	hip
la	**carne**	flesh
la	**columna (vertebral)**	spine
la	**costilla**	rib
la	**facción** *(pl* facciones)	feature
la	**mandíbula**	jaw
la	**muñeca**	wrist
la	**nuca**	nape of the neck
la	**pantorrilla**	calf *(of leg)*
la	**pestaña**	eyelash
la	**planta del pie**	sole of the foot
la	**pupila**	pupil *(of the eye)*
la	**sien**	temple *(of head)*
la	**talla**	size
la	**tez** *(pl* teces)	complexion
la	**uña**	nail
la	**vena**	vein

USEFUL PHRASES

contorno de caderas **hip measurement**
cintura **waist measurement**
contorno de pecho **chest measurement**
sordo(a) **deaf**
ciego(a) **blind**
mudo(a) **mute**
discapacitado(a) **disabled**
disminuido(a) psíquico(a) **person with learning difficulties**
él es más alto que tú **he is taller than you**
ella ha crecido mucho **she has grown a lot**
estoy demasiado gordo(a) *or* tengo sobrepeso **I am overweight**
ella ha engordado/adelgazado **she has put on/lost weight**
ella mide 1,47 metros **she is 1.47 metres tall**
él pesa 40 kilos **he weighs 40 kilos**

SEASONS

la	**primavera**	spring
el	**verano**	summer
el	**otoño**	autumn
el	**invierno**	winter

MONTHS

enero	January	**julio**	July
febrero	February	**agosto**	August
marzo	March	**septiembre**	September
abril	April	**octubre**	October
mayo	May	**noviembre**	November
junio	June	**diciembre**	December

DAYS OF THE WEEK

lunes	Monday
martes	Tuesday
miércoles	Wednesday
jueves	Thursday
viernes	Friday
sábado	Saturday
domingo	Sunday

USEFUL PHRASES

en primavera/verano/otoño/invierno in spring/summer/autumn/winter
en mayo in May
el 10 de julio de 2006 on 10 July 2006
es 3 de diciembre it's 3rd December
los sábados voy a la piscina on Saturdays I go to the swimming pool
el sábado fui a la piscina on Saturday I went to the swimming pool
el próximo sábado/el sábado pasado next/last Saturday
el sábado anterior/siguiente the previous/following Saturday

CALENDAR

el	calendario	calendar
el	día	day
los	días de la semana	days of the week
el	día festivo	public holiday
la	estación (*pl* estaciones)	season
el	mes	month
la	semana	week

USEFUL PHRASES

el día de los (Santos) Inocentes April Fools' Day (*celebrated on 28 December in Spain*)

la broma del día de los (Santos) Inocentes April fool's trick

el primero de mayo May Day

el día de la Hispanidad Columbus Day (*Spain's national day, celebrated on 12 October*)

el himno nacional de España Spain's national anthem

el día D D-Day

el día de San Valentín St Valentine's Day

el día de Todos los Santos All Saints' Day

la Semana Santa Easter

el Domingo de Resurrección *or* Pascua Easter Sunday

el Lunes de Pascua Easter Monday

el Miércoles de Ceniza Ash Wednesday

el Viernes Santo Good Friday

la Cuaresma Lent

la Pascua judía Passover

el Ramadán Ramadan

el Hanukkah Hanukkah *or* Hanukah

el Divali *or* el Festival de la Luz Divali *or* Diwali

el Adviento Advent

la Nochebuena Christmas Eve

la Navidad Christmas

en Navidad at Christmas

el día de Navidad Christmas Day

la Nochevieja New Year's Eve

el día de Año Nuevo New Year's Day

la cena *or* fiesta de Fin de Año New Year's Eve dinner *or* party

ESSENTIAL WORDS *(masculine)*

el	**aniversario de boda**	wedding anniversary
el	**cumpleaños** *(pl inv)*	birthday
el	**(día del) santo**	saint's day
el	**divorcio**	divorce
el	**matrimonio**	marriage
el	**regalo**	present

IMPORTANT WORDS *(masculine)*

el	**compromiso**	engagement
el	**festival**	festival
los	**fuegos artificiales**	fireworks; firework display
el	**nacimiento**	birth
el	**parque de atracciones**	fun fair

USEFUL WORDS *(masculine)*

el	**bautismo**	christening
el	**cementerio**	cemetery
el	**entierro**	funeral
el	**festival folclórico**	folk festival
el	**testigo**	witness
el	**regalo de Navidad**	Christmas present

USEFUL PHRASES

celebrar el cumpleaños to celebrate one's birthday
mi hermana nació en 1995 my sister was born in 1995
ella acaba de cumplir 17 años she's just turned 17
él me dio este regalo he gave me this present
¡te lo regalo! I'm giving it to you!
gracias thank you
divorciarse to get divorced
casarse to get married
comprometerse (con algn) to get engaged (to sb)
mi padre murió hace dos años my father died two years ago
enterrar to bury

ESSENTIAL WORDS (feminine)

la	boda	wedding
la	cita	appointment, date
la	fecha	date
la	fiesta	festival; fair; party

IMPORTANT WORDS (feminine)

las	fiestas	festivities
la	feria	fair
la	muerte	death
la	hoguera	bonfire

USEFUL WORDS (feminine)

la	ceremonia	ceremony
la	dama de honor	bridesmaid
la	invitación de boda (pl invitaciones ~~)	wedding invitation
la	jubilación (pl jubilaciones)	retirement
la	luna de miel	honeymoon
la	procesión (pl procesiones)	procession; march
la	tarjeta de felicitación	greetings card
la	testigo	witness

USEFUL PHRASES

bodas de plata/oro/diamante silver/golden/diamond wedding anniversary
desear a algn (un) Feliz Año to wish sb a happy New Year
dar or hacer una fiesta to have a party
invitar a los amigos to invite one's friends
elegir un regalo to choose a gift
¡Feliz navidad! or ¡Felices Pascuas! Happy Christmas!
¡Feliz cumpleaños! happy birthday!
(con) nuestros mejores deseos best wishes

ESSENTIAL WORDS (*masculine*)

los	aseos	toilets
los	baños (*LAm*)	washrooms; toilets
el	bote	tin, can
el	camping (*pl ~s*)	camping; campsite
el	campista	camper
el	cerillo (*LAm*)	match
el	cubo de la basura	dustbin
el	cuchillo	knife
el	depósito de butano	butane store
el	emplazamiento	pitch, site
el	espejo	mirror
el	gas	gas
el	guarda	warden
el	lavabo	washbasin
el	plato	plate
los	servicios (*Sp*)	washrooms; toilets
el	suplemento	extra charge
el	tenedor	fork
el	trailer (*pl ~s*) (*LAm*)	trailer
el	vehículo	vehicle

IMPORTANT WORDS (*masculine*)

el	abrelatas (*pl inv*)	tin-opener
el	colchón inflable (*pl* colchones ~s)	airbed
el	detergente	washing powder
el	enchufe	socket
el	hornillo	stove
el	sacacorchos (*pl inv*)	corkscrew
el	saco de dormir	sleeping bag

USEFUL PHRASES

ir de *or* hacer camping to go camping
acampar to camp
bien equipado(a) well equipped
hacer una hoguera to make a fire

ESSENTIAL WORDS *(feminine)*

el	**agua (no) potable** (*f*)	(non-)drinking water
la	**alberca** (*Mex*)	swimming pool
la	**caja**	box
la	**cama plegable**	camp bed
la	**campista**	camper
la	**caravana**	caravan; motorhome
la	**carpa** (*LAm*)	tent
la	**cerilla**	match
la	**comida enlatada**	tinned food
la	**cuchara**	spoon
la	**ducha**	shower
la	**hoguera de campamento**	campfire
la	**lata**	tin, can
la	**lavadora**	washing machine
la	**linterna**	torch
la	**mesa**	table
la	**navaja**	penknife
la	**noche**	night
la	**piscina** (*Sp*)	swimming pool
la	**sala**	room; hall
la	**tienda (de campaña)** (*Sp*)	tent
la	**tumbona**	deckchair

IMPORTANT WORDS *(feminine)*

la	**barbacoa**	barbecue
la	**colada**	washing
las	**instalaciones sanitarias**	washing facilities
la	**lavandería**	launderette
la	**mochila**	rucksack
las	**normas**	rules
la	**sala de juegos**	games room
la	**sombra**	shade; shadow
la	**toma de corriente**	socket

USEFUL PHRASES

montar una tienda **to pitch a tent**
asar unas salchichas (a la parrilla) **to grill some sausages**

ESSENTIAL WORDS (masculine)

el	aeromozo (LAm)	steward; flight attendant
el	agricultor	farmer
el	auxiliar de vuelo (Sp)	steward; flight attendant
el	banco	bank
el	bombero	fireman
el	cajero	check-out assistant
el	cartero	postman
el	diseñador de páginas web	web designer
el	electricista	electrician
el	empleado	employee
el	empresario	employer
el	enfermero	nurse
el	farmacéutico	chemist
el	informático	computer programmer
el	jefe	boss
el	maquinista	engineer; train driver
el	mecánico	mechanic
el	médico	doctor
el	minero	miner
el	oficio	trade
el	orientador profesional	careers adviser
el	policía	policeman
el	profesor	teacher
el	propietario de un taller (mecánico or de reparaciones)	garage owner
el	redactor	editor
el	soldado	soldier
el	sueldo	wages
el	taxista	taxi driver
el	trabajo	job; work
el	vendedor	sales assistant, shop assistant

USEFUL PHRASES

interesante/poco interesante interesting/not very interesting
él es cartero he is a postman; él/ella es médico he/she is a doctor
trabajar to work
hacerse, volverse to become

ESSENTIAL WORDS *(feminine)*

la	aeromoza *(LAm)*	stewardess; flight attendant
la	agricultora	farmer
la	ambición *(pl* ambiciones)	ambition
la	auxiliar de vuelo	stewardess; flight attendant
la	cajera	check-out assistant
la	cartera	postwoman
la	consejera profesional	careers adviser
la	empleada	employee
la	enfermera	nurse
la	estrella *(m+f)*	star
la	fábrica	factory
la	informática	computer programmer
la	jefa	boss
la	jubilación *(pl* jubilaciones)	retirement
la	mecanógrafa	typist
la	médico	doctor
la	oficina	office
la	profesión *(pl* profesiones)	profession
la	profesora	teacher
la	recepcionista	receptionist
la	redactora	editor
la	secretaria	secretary
la	vendedora	sales assistant, shop assistant
la	vida	life
la	vida laboral	working life

USEFUL PHRASES

trabajar para ganarse la vida to work for one's living
mi ambición es ser juez(a) it is my ambition to be a judge
¿en qué trabajas? what do you do (for a living)?
solicitar un trabajo to apply for a job

IMPORTANT WORDS *(masculine)*

el **aprendizaje**	apprenticeship
el **asalariado**	wage-earner
el **aumento**	rise
el **autor**	author
el **bombero**	fireman
el **colega**	colleague
el **comerciante**	shopkeeper
el **contrato**	contract
el **conserje**	caretaker
el **decorador**	decorator
el **desempleado**	unemployed person
el **desempleo**	unemployment
el **empleo**	job; situation
el **fontanero** (*Sp*)	plumber
el **futuro**	future
el **gerente**	manager
el **hombre de negocios**	businessman
el **INEM**	employment organization; institute of employment
el **interino**	temp
el **jefe**	boss
el **mercado laboral**	job market
el **negocio** *or* los **negocios**	business
el **óptico**	optician
el **peluquero**	hairdresser
el **piloto**	pilot
el **pintor**	painter
el **plomero** (*Mex*)	plumber
el **presidente**	president; chairperson
el **sindicato**	trade union
el **trabajador**	worker
el **trabajo**	job

USEFUL PHRASES

estar desempleado(a) *or* en paro **to be unemployed**
despedir a algn **to make sb redundant**
contrato indefinido/temporal/a término fijo **permanent/temporary/ fixed term contract**

IMPORTANT WORDS *(feminine)*

la	acomodadora	usher
la	agencia de trabajo temporal	temping agency
la	asalariada	wage-earner
la	biblioteca	library
la	carrera	career
la	carta adjunta	covering letter
la	cocinera	cook
la	colega	colleague
la	conserje	caretaker
la	entrevista (de trabajo)	(job) interview
la	gerente	manager
la	huelga	strike
la	interina	temp
la	limpiadora	cleaner
la	mujer de negocios	businesswoman
la	oficina de empleo	job centre
la	peluquera	hairdresser
la	pintora	painter
la	política	politics
la	presidenta	president; chairperson
la	solicitud	application
la	trabajadora	worker

USEFUL PHRASES

"demandas de empleo" "situations wanted"
"ofertas de empleo" "situations vacant"
estar en/pertenercer a un sindicato to be in a union
ganar 150 libras a la semana to earn £150 a week
una subida *or* un aumento de sueldo a pay rise
ponerse *or* declararse en huelga to go on strike
estar en huelga to be on strike
trabajar jornada completa/media jornada to work full-time/part-time
trabajar horas extra(s) to work overtime
reducción de la jornada laboral reduction in working hours

USEFUL WORDS *(masculine)*

el	abogado	lawyer
el	agente comercial	sales rep
el	albañil	mason
el	arquitecto	architect
el	artista	artist
el	carpintero	joiner
el	cirujano	surgeon
el	contable (*Sp*), el contador (*LAm*)	accountant
el	cosmonauta	cosmonaut
el	cura	priest
el	curso de formación	training course
el	diputado	MP
el	diseñador	fashion designer
el	ejecutivo	executive
el	escritor	writer
el	fotógrafo	photographer
el	funcionario	civil servant
el	horario	schedule
el	ingeniero	engineer
el	intérprete	interpreter
el	investigador	researcher
el	juez (*pl* jueces)	judge
el	marinero	sailor
el	modelo	model (*person*)
el	monitor de actividades	activity leader
el	negocio	business
el	notario	notary
el	paro	unemployment benefit
el	periodista	journalist
el	(período de) trabajo en prácticas	work placement
el	personal	staff
el	político	politician
el	director ejecutivo	managing director
el	procurador	solicitor
el	representante	rep; sales rep
el	sacerdote	priest
el	traductor	translator
el	veterinario	vet
el	viticultor	wine grower

USEFUL WORDS *(feminine)*

la	**abogada**	lawyer
la	**administración** (*pl* administraciones)	administration
el	**ama de casa** (*pl* f amas ~ ~)	housewife
la	**monitora de actividades**	activity leader
la	**artista**	artist
la	**compañía**	company
la	**contable** (*Sp*), la **contadora** (*LAm*)	accountant
la	**empresa**	company
la	**formación**	training
la	**funcionaria**	civil servant
la	**huelga de celo**	work-to-rule; go-slow
la	**indemnización por desempleo**	redundancy payment
la	**intérprete**	interpreter
la	**jueza**	judge
la	**locutora**	announcer
la	**modelo**	model (*person*)
la	**modista**	dressmaker
la	**monja**	nun
la	**orientación profesional**	careers guidance
la	**periodista**	journalist
la	**policía**	policewoman
la	**religiosa**	nun
la	**representante**	rep; sales rep
la	**taquimecanógrafa**	shorthand typist
la	**traductora**	translator

USEFUL PHRASES

el trabajo temporal **seasonal work**
un empleo temporal/permanente **a temporary/permanent job**
un trabajo a tiempo parcial (*Sp*) *or* a medio tiempo (*LAm*) **a part-time job**
ser contratado(a) **to be taken on**; ser despedido(a) **to be dismissed**
despedir *or* echar a algn **to give sb the sack**
buscar trabajo **to look for work**
hacer un curso de formación profesional **to go on a training course**
fichar al entrar a/al salir de trabajar **to clock in/out**
trabajar en horario flexible **to work flexitime**

ESSENTIAL WORDS *(masculine)*

el	aceite	oil
el	agente de policía	policeman
el	aparcamiento *(Sp)*	car park
el	atasco	traffic jam
el	autoestop	hitch-hiking
el	autoestopista	hitch-hiker
el	automóvil	car
el	aventón *(Mex)*	hitch-hiking
el	callejero	street map
el	camión *(pl* camiones*)*	lorry, truck
el	carnet *or* carné de conducir *(Sp) (pl* ~s *or* ~s ~ ~*)*	driving licence
el	carro *(LAm)*	car
el	ciclista	cyclist
el	coche *(Sp)*	car
el	conductor	driver
el	cruce	crossroads
el	chófer	driver; chauffeur
el	diesel	diesel
el	estacionamiento *(LAm)*	car park
los	faros	headlights
el	freno	brake
el	garaje	garage
el	gasoil	diesel *(oil)*
el	kilómetro	kilometre
el	litro	litre
el	mapa de carreteras	road map
el	mecánico	mechanic
el	neumático	tyre
el	número	number
el	parking *(pl* ~s*)*	car park
el	peaje	toll
el	peatón *(pl* peatones*)*	pedestrian
el	radar	speed camera
el	semáforo	traffic lights
el	trailer *(pl* ~s*) (LAm)*	caravan
el	viaje	journey

ESSENTIAL WORDS (feminine)

el	agua (f)	water
la	autoestopista	hitch-hiker
la	autopista	motorway
la	autopista de peaje	toll motorway
la	caravana (Sp)	caravan
la	carretera	road
la	carretera nacional	main road
la	ciclista	cyclist
la	cochera	garage
la	conductora	driver
la	chófer	driver; chauffeur
la	desviación (pl desviaciones)	diversion
la	dirección (pl direcciones)	direction
la	dirección asistida (pl direcciones ~s)	power steering
la	distancia	distance
la	estación de servicio (pl estaciones ~ ~)	petrol station
la	gasolina	petrol
la	gasolina sin plomo	unleaded petrol
la	libreta de manejar (Mex)	driving licence
la	matrícula (Sp), la placa (LAm)	(car) registration document
la	policía	police
la	póliza de seguros	insurance certificate

USEFUL PHRASES

frenar bruscamente to brake suddenly

100 kilómetros por hora 100 kilometres an hour

¿tienes carné (or carnet) de conducir? do you have a driving licence?

vamos a dar una vuelta (en coche) we're going for a drive (in the car)

¡lleno, por favor!, ¡llénelo, por favor! fill her up please!

tomar la carretera a/hacia Córdoba take the road to Córdoba

es un viaje de tres horas it's a 3-hour journey

¡buen viaje! have a good journey!

¡vámonos!, ¡en marcha! let's go!

de camino vimos … on the way we saw …

adelantar a un coche to overtake a car

IMPORTANT WORDS *(masculine)*

el	**accidente (de carretera)**	(road) accident
el	**aparcamiento**	parking
el	**atasco**	traffic jam
el	**camionero**	lorry driver
el	**choque**	collision
el	**cinturón de seguridad**	seat belt
	(*pl* cinturones ~ ~)	
el	**claxon** (*pl* cláxones *or* ~s)	horn
el	**código de la circulación**	highway code
el	**daño**	damage
el	**embrague**	clutch
el	**encargado de una gasolinera**	petrol pump attendant
el	**faro**	headlight
el	**maletero** (*Sp*)	boot
el	**motociclista**	motorcyclist
el	**motor**	engine
el	**motorista**	motorist
los	**papeles (del coche)**	official papers
el	**pinchazo**	puncture
el	**pito**	horn
el	**salpicadero**	dashboard
el	**seguro**	insurance
el	**surtidor (de gasolina)**	petrol pump
el	**tráfico**	traffic
el	**túnel de lavado de coches**	car wash

USEFUL PHRASES

primero enciendes *or* pones el motor en marcha first you switch on the engine

el motor arranca *or* se pone en marcha the engine starts up

el coche se pone en marcha the car moves off

estamos circulando we're driving along

acelerar to accelerate; continuar to continue

reducir *or* aminorar la velocidad *or* la marcha to slow down

detenerse to stop; aparcar (el coche) to park (the car)

apagar el motor to switch off the engine

parar con el semáforo en rojo to stop at the red light

IMPORTANT WORDS *(feminine)*

la	autoescuela (*Sp*)	driving school
la	avería	breakdown
la	batería	battery
la	cajuela (*Mex*)	boot
la	calle de sentido único	one-way street
la	carrocería	body work
la	colisión (*pl* colisiones)	collision
la	documentación (del coche)	official papers
la	esculela de conductores (*LAm*) or de manejo (*Mex*)	driving school
la	frontera	border
la	glorieta	roundabout
la	grúa	breakdown van
la	ITV (inspección técnica de vehículos) (*Sp*)	MOT test
la	marca	make (*of car*)
la	motociclista	motorcyclist
la	motorista	motorist
la	pieza de repuesto	spare part
la	póliza de seguros	insurance policy
la	prioridad	right of way
la	prueba del alcohol	Breathalyser® test
la	puerta	(*car*) door
la	rotonda	roundabout
la	rueda	tyre
la	rueda de repuesto	spare tyre
la	velocidad	speed; gear
la	zona azul	restricted parking zone

USEFUL PHRASES

ha habido un accidente there's been an accident
hubo seis heridos en el accidente six people were injured in the accident
¿puedo ver la documentación *or* los papeles del coche, por favor? may I see your papers please?
pinchar, tener un pinchazo to have a puncture; arreglar to fix
averiarse *or* tener una avería to break down
me he quedado sin gasolina I've run out of petrol

USEFUL WORDS *(masculine)*

el	**acelerador**	accelerator
el	**arcén** *(pl arcenes)*	hard shoulder
el	**autolavado**	car-wash
el	**botón de arranque** *(pl botones ~ ~)*	starter
el	**capó**	bonnet
el	**carburador**	carburettor
el	**carril**	lane
el	**catalizador**	catalytic converter
el	**conductor novel**	learner driver
el	**consumo de gasolina**	petrol consumption
el	**cuentakilómetros** *(pl inv)*	speedometer
el	**desvío**	detour
el	**guardia de tráfico**	traffic warden
el	**herido**	casualty
el	**intermitente**	indicator
el	**lavacoches** *(pl inv)*	car-wash
el	**límite de velocidad**	speed limit
el	**limpiaparabrisas** *(pl inv)*	windscreen wiper
el	**parabrisas** *(pl inv)*	windscreen
el	**parachoques** *(pl inv)*	bumper
el	**parquímetro**	parking meter
el	**pedal**	pedal
el	**policía motorizado**	motorcycle policeman
el	**profesor de autoescuela**	driving instructor
el	**remolque**	trailer
el	**retrovisor**	rear-view mirror
el	**(sistema de navegación) GPS**	satellite navigation system
el	**volante**	steering wheel

USEFUL PHRASES

en la hora punta **at rush hour**
le pusieron una multa de 100 euros **he got a 100-euro fine**
¿está asegurado? **are you insured?**
no olviden ponerse los cinturones de seguridad **don't forget to put on your seat belts**
en la frontera **at the border**
hacer autoestop **to hitch-hike**

USEFUL WORDS (feminine)

el	**área de descanso** (pl f las áreas ~ ~)	lay-by
el	**área de servicio** (pl f las áreas ~ ~)	service area
la	**baca**	roof rack
la	**caja de cambios**	gearbox
la	**carretera de circunvalación**	ring road
la	**clase de conducir**	driving lesson
la	**curva**	bend
la	**estación de servicio** (pl estaciones ~ ~)	filling station
la	**gasolinera**	filling station
la	**guardia de tráfico**	traffic warden
la	**infracción de tráfico** (pl infracciones ~ ~)	traffic offence
la	**matrícula**	number plate
la	**mediana**	central reservation
la	**multa**	fine
la	**parada de emergencia**	emergency stop
la	**presión**	pressure
la	**señal de tráfico**	road sign
la	**vía**	way, road; lane (on road)
la	**vía de acceso**	slip road
la	**víctima** (m+f)	casualty
la	**zona urbanizada**	built-up area

USEFUL PHRASES

la rueda delantera/trasera the front/back wheel
tenemos que desviarnos we have to make a detour
una multa por exceso de velocidad a fine for speeding
contratar a un conductor to book a driver

"ceda el paso a la derecha" "give way to the right"
"circule por la derecha" "keep to the right"
"prohibido el paso" "no entry"
"prohibido aparcar" "no parking"
"obras" "roadworks"

ESSENTIAL WORDS (masculine)

el	abrigo	overcoat; coat
el	anorak (pl inv or ~s)	anorak
el	bañador	swimming trunks; swimsuit
el	bolso	bag
el	botón (pl botones)	button
el	calcetín (pl calcetines)	sock
los	calzoncillos	pants; boxer shorts
los	calzones (LAm)	knickers
el	camisón (pl camisones)	nightdress
el	chubasquero	raincoat
el	cuello	collar
el	jersey (pl ~s)	jumper
el	número (de pie)	(shoe) size
el	pantalón (pl pantalones)	trousers
los	(pantalones) vaqueros	jeans
el	pañuelo	handkerchief
el	paraguas (pl inv)	umbrella
el	pijama	pyjamas
el	sombrero	hat
el	talle	waist
el	traje	suit (for man); costume
el	traje de chaqueta	suit
el	vestido	dress
el	zapato	shoe

IMPORTANT WORDS (masculine)

el	bolsillo	pocket
el	bolso	handbag
el	cinturón (pl cinturones)	belt
el	guante	glove
el	impermeable	raincoat
los	pantalones cortos	shorts
el	uniforme	uniform

ESSENTIAL WORDS *(feminine)*

la	braga (del bikini)	bikini bottoms
las	bragas *(Sp)*	pants; knickers
la	camisa	shirt
la	camiseta	T-shirt
la	capucha	hood
la	chaqueta	jacket
la	corbata	tie
la	falda	skirt
las	medias	tights
la	moda	fashion
la	parka	parka
la	ropa	clothes
la	ropa interior	underwear
la	sandalia	sandal
la	talla	size

IMPORTANT WORDS *(feminine)*

la	americana	jacket *(for man)*
la	blusa	blouse
la	bota	boot
las	prendas de vestir	clothes
la	zapatilla	slipper

USEFUL PHRASES

por la mañana me visto in the morning I get dressed
por la tarde me desvisto in the evening I get undressed
cuando llego a casa del colegio me cambio when I get home from school
   I get changed
llevar, llevar puesto to wear
ponerse to put on
eso es muy elegante that's very smart
(eso) te queda bien that suits you
¿qué talla tienes (or tiene)? what size do you take?
¿qué número de pie tienes (or tiene)? what shoe size do you take?
tengo un 38 (de pie), calzo un 38 I take size 38 in shoes

USEFUL WORDS (*masculine*)

los	**accesorios**	accessories
el	**bastón** (*pl* bastones)	walking stick
el	**bolso bandolera** (*pl* ~s ~)	shoulder bag
el	**cárdigan** (*pl* ~s)	cardigan
el	**chaleco**	vest; waistcoat
el	**chándal** (*pl* ~s)	tracksuit
los	**cordones**	(shoe)laces
el	**delantal**	apron
el	**desfile de moda**	fashion show
el	**foulard** (*pl* ~s)	scarf
el	**lazo**	ribbon
el	**mono**	overalls
el	**ojal**	buttonhole
los	**pantis**	tights
el	**pañuelo**	scarf
el	**peto**	overalls; dungarees
el	**polar**	fleece
el	**polo**	polo shirt
el	**probador**	fitting room
el	**sujetador**	bra
el	**traje de chaqueta**	suit (*for woman*)
el	**traje de etiqueta**	evening dress (*for man*)
el	**traje de noche**	evening dress (*for woman*)
el	**traje pantalón** (*pl* ~s ~)	trouser suit
los	**tirantes**	braces
el	**vestido de novia**	wedding dress
los	**zapatos de tacón**	high heels
los	**zapatos de tacón de aguja**	stiletto heels

USEFUL WORDS *(feminine)*

la	alpargata	espadrille
la	alta costura	haute couture
la	bandolera	shoulder bag
la	bata	dressing gown
las	bermudas	Bermuda shorts
la	boina	beret
la	bufanda	scarf
la	camiseta con capucha	hooded top
la	camiseta sin mangas	tank top
las	chanclas	flip flops
la	cinta	ribbon
la	colada	washing
la	combinación (*pl* combinaciones)	underskirt
la	cremallera	zip
la(s)	enagua(s)	underskirt
la	falda pantalón (*pl* ~s ~)	culottes
la	gorra	cap
la	limpieza en seco	dry-cleaning
la	manga	sleeve
las	medias	stockings
la	pajarita	bow tie
la	rebeca	cardigan
la	ropa blanca	washing
la	sudadera	sweatshirt
las	zapatillas de deporte	trainers

USEFUL PHRASES

largo(a) long; corto(a) short
un vestido de manga corta/larga a short-sleeved/long-sleeved dress
estrecho(a), ajustado(a) tight
amplio(a), suelto(a) loose
una falda ajustada *or* ceñida a tight skirt
a rayas, de rayas striped; a cuadros, de cuadros checked; de lunares spotted
ropa de sport, ropa informal casual clothes
con vestido de noche in evening dress
a la moda, de moda fashionable; moderno(a) trendy
pasado(a) de moda, anticuado(a) old-fashioned

amarillo(a)	yellow
azul	blue
azul celeste	sky blue
azul claro	pale blue
azul marino	navy blue
azul oscuro	dark blue
azul real	royal blue
beige, beis	beige
blanco(a)	white
burdeos (*pl inv*)	maroon
crudo(a)	natural
dorado(a)	golden
granate	maroon
gris	grey
malva	mauve
marrón (*pl* marrones)	brown
morado(a)	purple
naranja	orange
negro(a)	black
rojo(a)	red
rojo fuerte *or* intenso	bright red
rosa	pink
turquesa	turquoise
verde	green
violeta	violet

USEFUL PHRASES

el color colour

¿de qué color tienes (or tiene) los ojos/el pelo? what colour are your eyes/ is your hair?

el azul te sienta bien blue suits you; the blue one suits you

pintar algo de azul to paint sth blue

los zapatos azules blue shoes

los zapatos azul claro light blue shoes

(ella) tiene los ojos verdes she has green eyes

cambiar de color to change colour

la Casa Blanca the White House

un (hombre) blanco a white man

una (mujer) blanca a white woman

un (hombre) negro a black man

una (mujer) negra a black woman

blanco como la nieve as white as snow

Blancanieves Snow White

Caperucita Roja Little Red Riding Hood

ponerse colorado(a) or rojo(a) to turn red

sonrojarse de vergüenza to blush with shame

blanco(a) como el papel as white as a sheet

muy moreno(a), muy bronceado(a) as brown as a berry

(él) estaba cubierto de cardenales he was black and blue

un ojo morado a black eye

un filete muy poco hecho a very rare steak, an underdone steak

ESSENTIAL WORDS *(masculine)*

el	**ordenador (personal)**	(personal) computer
el	**programa**	program
el	**programador**	programmer
el	**ratón** *(pl* ratones)	mouse

USEFUL WORDS *(masculine)*

el	**cartucho de tinta**	ink cartridge
el	**CD-ROM** *(pl inv)*	CD-ROM
el	**corrector ortográfico**	spellchecker
el	**correo electrónico**	email
el	**cursor**	cursor
los	**datos**	data
el	**disco duro**	hard disk
el	**disquete**	floppy disk
el	**documento**	document
el	**fichero**	file
el	**icono**	icon
el	**internauta**	internet user
el	**Internet**	internet
el	**juego de ordenador**	computer game
el	**mail** *(pl ~s)*	email
el	**menú**	menu
el	**módem** *(pl ~s)*	modem
el	**monitor**	monitor
el	**navegador**	browser
el	**ordenador portátil**	laptop
el	**paquete de programas**	software package
el	**pirata informático**	hacker
el	**procesador de textos**	wordprocessor
el	**servidor**	server
el	**sitio web**	website
el	**software** *(pl inv)*	software
el	**soporte (físico)**	hardware
el	**teclado**	keyboard
el	**virus** *(pl inv)*	virus
el	**Web** *(pl ~s)*	Web
el	**wifi**	wifi

ESSENTIAL WORDS *(feminine)*

la	**impresora**	printer
la	**informática**	computer science; computer studies

USEFUL WORDS *(feminine)*

la	**aplicación** (*pl* aplicaciones)	program
la	**banda ancha**	broadband
la	**base de datos**	database
la	**computadora (personal)** (*LAm*)	(personal) computer
la	**copia de seguridad**	back-up
la	**copia impresa**	print-out
la	**dirección de correo (electrónico)** (*pl* direcciones ~ ~ (~))	e-mail address
la	**función** (*pl* funciones)	function
la	**grabadora de DVD**	DVD writer
la	**hoja de cálculo**	spreadsheet
la	**interfaz** (*pl* interfaces)	interface
la	**internauta**	internet user
la	**Internet**	Internet
la	**llave USB**	USB key
la	**memoria**	memory
la	**memoria RAM**	RAM, random-access memory
la	**memoria ROM**	ROM, read-only Memory
la	**página de inicio**	home page
la	**pantalla**	screen
la	**papelera de reciclaje**	recycle bin
la	**red**	network
la	**unidad de disco**	disk drive
la	**ventana**	window
la	**Web** (*pl* ~s)	Web
la	**webcam** (*pl* ~s)	webcam

USEFUL PHRASES

copiar to copy; eliminar, suprimir to delete; formatear to format
descargar un archivo to download a file
guardar to save; imprimir to print; teclear to key
navegar por Internet to surf the internet

COUNTRIES

ESSENTIAL WORDS (*masculine*)

Canadá	Canada
EE.UU.	USA
Estados Unidos	United States
país	country
Países Bajos	Netherlands
Reino Unido	United Kingdom

USEFUL WORDS (*masculine*)

Brasil	Brazil
Ecuador	Ecuador
El Salvador	El Salvador
Japón	Japan
Marruecos	Morocco
México	Mexico
Pakistán	Pakistan
Panamá	Panama
Paraguay	Paraguay
Perú	Peru
Tercer Mundo	Third World
Túnez	Tunisia
Uruguay	Uruguay

USEFUL PHRASES

mi país de origen my native country
la capital de España the capital of Spain
¿de qué país eres (*or* es)? what country do you come from?
soy de (los) Estados Unidos/de Canadá I come from the United States/ from Canada
nací en Escocia I was born in Scotland
me voy a los Países Bajos I'm going to the Netherlands
acabo de regresar de (los) Estados Unidos I have just come back from the United States
los países en (vías de) desarrollo the developing countries
países de habla hispana Spanish-speaking countries

ESSENTIAL WORDS *(feminine)*

América	America
América del Sur	South America
Alemania	Germany
Bélgica	Belgium
Escocia	Scotland
España	Spain
Europa	Europe
Francia	France
Gran Bretaña	Great Britain
Holanda	Holland
Inglaterra	England
Irlanda (del Norte)	(Northern) Ireland
Italia	Italy
(el País de) Gales	Wales
Sudamérica	South America
Suiza	Switzerland
USA	USA

USEFUL WORDS *(feminine)*

África	Africa
Argelia	Algeria
Asia	Asia
Bolivia	Bolivia
Colombia	Colombia
Costa Rica	Costa Rica
Cuba	Cuba
Francia	France
Grecia	Greece
Guatemala	Guatemala
la India	India
Nicaragua	Nicaragua
la República Dominicana	the Dominican Republic
la Unión Europea, UE	the European Union, the EU
Venezuela	Venezuela

NATIONALITIES

ESSENTIAL WORDS (*masculine*)

un **alemán** (*pl* alemanes)	a German
un **americano**	an American
un **belga**	a Belgian
un **británico**	a Briton
un **canadiense**	a Canadian
un **escocés** (*pl* escoceses)	a Scot
un **español**	a Spaniard
un **europeo**	a European
un **francés** (*pl* franceses)	a Frenchman
un **galés** (*pl* galeses)	a Welshman
un **holandés** (*pl* holandeses)	a Dutchman
un **inglés** (*pl* ingleses)	an Englishman
un **irlandés** (*pl* irlandeses)	an Irishman
un **italiano**	an Italian
un **pakistaní** (*pl* ~es *or* ~s)	a Pakistani
un **suizo**	a Swiss (man *or* boy)

USEFUL PHRASES

(él) es irlandés he is Irish
(ella) es irlandesa she is Irish
la campiña irlandesa the Irish countryside
una ciudad irlandesa an Irish town

ESSENTIAL WORDS *(feminine)*

una	**alemana**	a German
una	**americana**	an American
una	**belga**	a Belgian
una	**británica**	a Briton, a British woman *or* girl
una	**canadiense**	a Canadian
una	**escocesa**	a Scot
una	**española**	a Spaniard
una	**europea**	a European
una	**francesa**	a Frenchwoman, a French girl
una	**galesa**	a Welshwoman, a Welsh girl
una	**holandesa**	a Dutchwoman, a Dutch girl
una	**inglesa**	an Englishwoman, an English girl
una	**irlandesa**	an Irishwoman, an Irish girl
una	**italiana**	an Italian
una	**pakistaní** (*pl* ~es *or* ~s)	a Pakistani
una	**suiza**	a Swiss girl *or* woman

USEFUL PHRASES

soy escocés – hablo inglés **I am Scottish – I speak English**
soy escocesa **I am Scottish**
un(a) extranjero(a) **a foreigner**
en el extranjero **abroad**
la nacionalidad **nationality**

USEFUL WORDS (*masculine*)

un	africano	an African
un	antillano	a West Indian
un	árabe	an Arab
un	argelino	an Algerian
un	argentino	an Argentinian
un	boliviano	a Bolivian
un	brasileño	a Brazilian
un	chileno	a Chilean
un	chino	a Chinese
un	colombiano	a Colombian
un	costarricense	a Costa Rican
un	cubano	a Cuban
un	dominicano	a Dominican
un	ecuatoriano	an Ecuadorean
un	griego	a Greek
un	guatemalteco	a Guatemalan
un	indio	an Indian
un	japonés (*pl* japoneses)	a Japanese
un	marroquí (*pl* ~es *or* ~s)	a Moroccan
un	mexicano	a Mexican
un	nicaragüense	a Nicaraguan
un	panameño	a Panamanian
un	paraguayo	a Paraguayan
un	peruano	a Peruvian
un	ruso	a Russian
un	salvadoreño	a Salvadorian
un	tunecino	a Tunisian
un	turco	a Turk
un	uruguayo	a Uruguayan
un	venezolano	a Venezuelan

USEFUL WORDS *(feminine)*

una	africana	an African
una	antillana	a West Indian
una	árabe	an Arab
una	argelina	an Algerian
una	argentina	an Argentinian
una	boliviana	a Bolivian
una	brasileña	a Brazilian
una	chilena	a Chilean
una	china	a Chinese
una	colombiana	a Colombian
una	costarricense	a Costa Rican
una	cubana	a Cuban
una	dominicana	a Dominican
una	ecuatoriana	an Ecuadorean
una	griega	a Greek
una	guatemalteca	a Guatemalan
una	india	an Indian
una	japonesa	a Japanese
una	marroquí *(pl ~es or ~s)*	a Moroccan
una	mexicana	a Mexican
una	nicaragüense	a Nicaraguan
una	panameña	a Panamanian
una	paraguaya	a Paraguayan
una	peruana	a Peruvian
una	rusa	a Russian
una	salvadoreña	a Salvadorian
una	tunecina	a Tunisian
una	turca	a Turk
una	uruguaya	a Uruguayan
una	venezolana	a Venezuelan

ESSENTIAL WORDS *(masculine)*

el	**aire**	air
el	**albergue juvenil**	youth hostel
el	**árbol**	tree
el	**arroyo**	stream
el	**bastón** (*pl* bastones)	walking stick
el	**bosque**	wood; forest
el	**camino**	way
el	**campesino**	countryman; farmer
el	**campo**	country; countryside
el	**castillo**	castle
el	**cazador**	hunter
el	**granjero**	farmer
el	**mercado**	market
el	**paisaje**	scenery
el	**paseo**	walk
el	**picnic** (*pl inv or* ~s)	picnic
el	**prado**	field
el	**pueblo**	village
el	**puente**	bridge
el	**río**	river
el	**ruido**	noise
el	**sendero**	path; track
el	**terreno**	soil; ground
el	**turista**	tourist
el	**valle**	valley

USEFUL PHRASES

al aire libre **in the open air**

sé el camino al pueblo **I know the way to the village**

salir en bicicleta **to go cycling**

los vecinos *or* los habitantes de la zona **the locals**

fuimos de picnic **we went for a picnic**

ESSENTIAL WORDS (feminine)

la	**barrera**	gate; fence
la	**camioneta** (*Sp*)	van
la	**campesina**	countrywoman; farmer
la	**carretera**	road
la	**cazadora**	hunter
la	**excursión** (*pl* excursiones)	hike
la	**granja**	farm, farmhouse
la	**granjera**	farmer
la	**montaña**	mountain
la	**piedra**	stone; rock
la	**región** (*pl* regiones)	district
la	**tierra**	land; earth; soil; ground
la	**torre**	tower
la	**turista**	tourist
la	**vagoneta** (*Mex*)	van
la	**valla**	fence

USEFUL PHRASES

en el campo **in the country**
ir (de excursión) al campo **to go into the country**
vivir en el campo/en la ciudad **to live in the country/in town**
cultivar la tierra **to cultivate the land**

IMPORTANT WORDS (masculine)

el	agricultor (Sp)	farmer
el	guardia civil	civil guard (person)
el	lago	lake
el	mesón (pl mesones)	inn
el	polvo	dust
el	ranchero (Mex)	farmer

USEFUL WORDS (masculine)

los	anteojos de larga vista (LAm)	binoculars
el	arbusto	bush
el	barro	mud
el	brezo	heather
el	charco	puddle
el	estanque	pond
el	guijarro	pebble
el	heno	hay
el	matorral	bush
el	molino (de viento)	(wind)mill
el	palo	stick
el	pantano	marsh
el	páramo	moor
el	poste telegráfico	telegraph pole
el	prado	meadow
los	prismáticos (Sp)	binoculars
el	seto	hedge
el	trigo	corn; wheat

USEFUL PHRASES

agrícola agricultural
apacible, tranquilo(a) peaceful
en la cima de la colina at the top of the hill
caer en una trampa to fall into a trap

IMPORTANT WORDS *(feminine)*

la **agricultora** *(Sp)*	farmer
la **agricultura**	agriculture
la **calzada**	road surface
la **catiusca, katiuska**	(wellington) boot
la **cima**	top *(of hill)*
la **colina**	hill
la **gente del campo**	country people
la **guardia civil**	civil guard *(person)*
la **Guardia Civil**	Civil Guard
la **hoja**	leaf
la **posada**	inn
la **propiedad**	property; estate
la **ranchera** *(Mex)*	farmer
la **tranquilidad**	peace

USEFUL WORDS *(feminine)*

la **aldea**	hamlet
la **bota de goma**	(wellington) boot
la **cantera**	quarry
la **cascada**	waterfall
la **caverna**	cave
la **caza**	hunting; shooting
la **cosecha**	crop; harvest
la **fuente**	spring; source
la **furgoneta**	van
la **llanura**	plain
la **orilla**	bank *(of river)*
las **ruinas**	ruins
la **señal**	signpost
la **trampa**	trap
la **vendimia**	grape harvest
la **zanja**	ditch

USEFUL PHRASES

perderse to lose one's way
recoger la cosecha to bring in the harvest
vendimiar, hacer la vendimia to harvest the grapes

ESSENTIAL WORDS *(masculine)*

el	**aspecto**	appearance
el	**bigote**	moustache
el	**cabello**	hair
el	**color**	colour
los	**ojos**	eyes
el	**talle**	waist

USEFUL PHRASES

alegre **cheerful**
alto(a) **tall**
amable **nice**
antiguo(a) **old**
asqueroso(a) **disgusting**
bajo(a) **short**
barbudo(a), con barba **bearded, with a beard**
bonito(a) **pretty**
bueno(a) **kind**
calvo(a) **bald**
delgado(a) **skinny**
desagradable **unpleasant**
dinámico(a) **dynamic**
divertido(a), entretenido(a) **amusing, entertaining**
educado(a) **polite**
esbelto(a) **slim**
estupendo(a) **great**
feliz (*pl* felices) **happy**
feo(a) **ugly**
gordo(a) **fat**
gracioso(a) **funny**
grosero(a) **rude**
guapo **handsome**; guapa **beautiful**
horrible **hideous**
infeliz (*pl* infelices), desgraciado(a) **unhappy, unfortunate**
inquieto(a) **agitated**
inteligente **intelligent**

ESSENTIAL WORDS *(feminine)*

la	**barba**	beard
la	**edad**	age
la	**estatura**	height; size
las	**gafas**	glasses
la	**identidad**	ID
la	**lágrima**	tear
la	**persona**	person
la	**talla**	size; height

USEFUL PHRASES

joven (*pl* jóvenes) **young**

largo(a) **long**

malo(a) **naughty**

mono(a) **cute**

nervioso(a), tenso(a) **nervous, tense**

optimista/pesimista **optimistic/pessimistic**

pequeño(a) **small, little**

que se porta bien **well-behaved**

serio(a) **serious**

tímido(a) **shy**

tonto(a) **stupid**

tranquilo(a) **calm**

viejo(a) **old**

(ella) parece triste **she looks sad**

(él) estaba llorando **he was crying**

(él) sonreía **he was smiling**

(él) tenía lágrimas en los ojos **he had tears in his eyes**

un hombre de estatura mediana **a man of average height**

mido 1 metro 70 *or* uno setenta *or* 1,70 **I am 1 metre 70 tall**

¿de qué color son tus (*or* sus) ojos/es tu (*or* su) pelo? **what colour are your eyes/is your hair?**

tengo el pelo rubio **I have fair hair**

tengo los ojos azules/verdes **I have blue/green eyes**

pelo moreno *or* castaño **dark *or* brown hair**

pelo castaño **light brown hair**; pelo rizado **curly hair**; pelirrojo(a) **red-haired**

pelo negro/canoso **black/grey hair**

pelo teñido **dyed hair**

IMPORTANT WORDS *(masculine)*

el	**carácter** (*pl* caracteres)	character; nature
el	**grano**	spot
el	**humor**	mood

USEFUL WORDS *(masculine)*

el	**cerquillo** (*LAm*)	fringe
el	**defecto**	fault
el	**fleco** (*Mex*), el **flequillo** (*Sp*)	fringe
el	**gesto**	gesture
el	**gigante**	giant
los	**hoyuelos**	dimples
el	**lunar**	mole, beauty spot
el	**parecido**	resemblance
el	**peso**	weight
el	**rizo**	curl

USEFUL PHRASES

(él) tiene buen carácter he is good-tempered
(él) tiene mal genio *or* carácter he is bad-tempered
tener la tez pálida *or* muy blanca to have a pale complexion
llevar gafas/lentes de contacto *or* lentillas to wear glasses/contact lenses

IMPORTANT WORDS *(feminine)*

la	**belleza**	beauty
la	**calidad**	(good) quality
la	**costumbre**	habit
la	**curiosidad**	curiosity
la	**expresión** *(pl* expresiones)	expression
la	**fealdad**	ugliness
las	**lentillas**	contact lenses
la	**mirada**	look
la	**sonrisa**	smile
la	**tez** *(pl* teces)	complexion
la	**voz** *(pl* voces)	voice

USEFUL WORDS *(feminine)*

las	**arrugas**	wrinkles
la	**cicatriz** *(pl* cicatrices)	scar
la	**dentadura (postiza)**	false teeth
las	**pecas**	freckles
la	**permanente**	perm
la	**timidez**	shyness

USEFUL PHRASES

siempre estoy de buen humor I am always in a good mood

(él) está de mal humor he is in a bad mood

(él) se enfadó he got angry

(ella) se parece a su madre she looks like her mother

(él) se muerde las uñas he bites his nails

ESSENTIAL WORDS (*masculine*)

el	**alemán**	German
el	**alfabeto**	alphabet
el	**alumno**	pupil; schoolboy
el	**amigo**	pal
el	**aprendizaje**	apprenticeship
el	**club** (*pl* ~s *or* ~es)	club
el	**colegio**	school
el	**colegio de secundaria**	secondary school
el	**comedor**	dining hall
el	**comienzo del curso**	beginning of term
el	**compañero de clase**	school friend
el	**concierto**	concert
el	**cuaderno**	notebook; exercise book
los	**deberes**	homework
el	**día**	day
el	**dibujo**	drawing
el	**director**	headmaster
el	**dormitorio**	dormitory
el	**error**	mistake
el	**escolar**	schoolboy
el	**español**	Spanish
el	**estudiante**	student
el	**estudio (de)**	study (of)
los	**estudios**	studies
el	**examen** (*pl* exámenes)	exam
el	**examen de prueba** (*pl* exámenes ~~)	mock exam
el	**experimento**	experiment
el	**fallo**	mistake
el	**francés**	French
el	**gimnasio**	gym
el	**grupo**	group
el	**horario**	timetable
el	**IES (Instituto de Enseñanza Secundaria)**	comprehensive school
el	**inglés**	English
el	**instituto**	secondary school
el	**intercambio**	exchange
el	**italiano**	Italian

ESSENTIAL WORDS *(feminine)*

la	alberca (*Mex*)	swimming pool
la	alumna	pupil; schoolgirl
la	amiga	pal
el	aula (*pl f* las aulas)	classroom
la	biología	biology
la	cafetería	canteen
las	ciencias	science
la	clase	class; year; classroom
las	clases	lessons
las	clases prácticas	practical class
la	compañera de clase	school friend
la	directora	headmistress
la	educación física	PE
la	electrónica	electronics
la	enseñanza	education; teaching
la	escolar	schoolgirl
la	escuela	school
la	escuela de primaria	primary school
la	escuela infantil	nursery school
la	estudiante	student
la	excursión (*pl* excursiones)	trip; outing
la	exposición (*pl* exposiciones)	presentation
la	física	physics
la	frase	sentence
la	geografía	geography
la	gimnasia	gym
la	goma (de borrar)	rubber
la	grabadora	tape recorder
la	guardería	nursery school
la	historia	history; story
la	informática	computer studies
la	lección (*pl* lecciones)	lesson
la	lectura	reading
las	lenguas (modernas)	(modern) languages
la	maestra de primaria *or* de infantil	primary schoolteacher
las	matemáticas	mathematics
la	materia (escolar)	(school) subject

ESSENTIAL WORDS (*masculine continued*)

el	**laboratorio**	laboratory
el	**lápiz** (*pl* lápices)	pencil
el	**libro**	book
el	**maestro de primaria** *or* **de infantil**	primary schoolteacher
el	**mapa**	map
el	**ordenador**	computer
el	**premio**	prize
el	**profesor**	teacher
el	**progreso**	progress
el	**recreo**	break; playtime
el	**resultado**	result
el	**semestre**	semester
el	**trabajo**	work
los	**trabajos manuales**	handicrafts

USEFUL PHRASES

trabajar to work
aprender to learn
estudiar to study
¿cuánto tiempo llevas (*or* lleva) aprendiendo español? how long have you been learning Spanish?
aprenderse algo de memoria to learn sth off by heart
tengo deberes/tareas todos los días *or* a diario I have homework every day
mi hermana pequeña va a primaria/al colegio – yo voy a secundaria *or* al instituto my little sister goes to primary school – I go to secondary school
enseñar español to teach Spanish
el/la profesor(a) de alemán the German teacher
he mejorado en matemáticas I have made progress in maths
hacer un examen to sit an exam
aprobar un examen to pass an exam
suspender un examen to fail an exam
sacar un aprobado to get a pass mark

ESSENTIAL WORDS *(feminine continued)*

las	**mates**	maths
la	**música**	music
la	**natación**	swimming
la	**nota**	mark
la	**palabra**	word
la	**piscina**	swimming pool
la	**pizarra**	blackboard
la	**pregunta**	question
la	**profesora**	teacher
la	**química**	chemistry
la	**respuesta**	answer
la	**sala de profesores**	staffroom
la	**tarea**	homework; task
la	**universidad**	university
las	**vacaciones**	holidays
las	**vacaciones de verano**	summer holidays

USEFUL PHRASES

fácil easy; difícil difficult

interesante interesting

aburrido(a) boring

leer to read; escribir to write

escuchar to listen (to)

mirar to look at, watch

repetir to repeat

responder to reply

hablar to speak

es la primera or mejor de la clase she is top of the class

es la última or peor de la clase she is bottom of the class

entrar en clase to go into the classroom

cometer un error or fallo to make a mistake

corregir to correct

cometí un error gramatical I made a grammatical error

he sacado buena nota I got a good mark

¡responde a la pregunta! answer the question!

¡levantad la mano! put your hand up!

IMPORTANT WORDS *(masculine)*

el bachillerato, el bachiller	higher school-leaving course/certificate
el certificado	certificate
el colegio concertado	grant-aided school
el colegio privado	private school
el colegio público	state school
el despacho	office
el día libre	day off
el diploma	diploma
el estuche	pencil case
el examen escrito *(pl* exámenes ~s)	written exam
el examen oral *(pl* exámenes ~es)	oral exam
el expediente	file
el papel	paper
el pasillo	corridor
el patio (de recreo)	playground

USEFUL PHRASES

mi amigo se está preparando la selectividad **my friend is sitting his university entrance exam**

repasar (la lección) **to revise**

repasaré otra vez la lección mañana **I'll go over the lesson again tomorrow**

IMPORTANT WORDS *(feminine)*

la	**ausencia**	absence
la	**carpeta**	folder; file
la	**conferencia**	lecture
las	**normas**	rules
las	**notas**	report
la	**oposición** *(pl* oposiciones)	competitive exam
la	**regla**	rule; ruler
la	**selectividad** *(Sp)*	entrance examination
la	**traducción** *(pl* traducciones)	translation
la	**versión** *(pl* versiones)	translation *(from foreign language to English)*

USEFUL PHRASES

en segundo de primaria **in year two**
en primero de ESO **in year seven**
en segundo de ESO **in year eight**
en tercero de ESO **in year nine**
en cuarto de ESO **in year ten**
en primero de bachillerato **in year eleven**

presente **present**
ausente **absent**
castigar a un(a) alumno(a) **to punish a pupil**
el/la profesor(a) los castigó sin recreo **the teacher kept them in at break time**
¡silencio!, ¡callaos! **be quiet!**

USEFUL WORDS *(masculine)*

el	**bedel**	janitor
el	**bloc** (*pl* ~s)	jotter
el	**boli, bolígrafo**	Biro®
el	**borrador**	rough copy
el	**cálculo**	sum
el	**castigo**	detention; punishment
el	**comportamiento**	behaviour
el	**corrector (líquido)**	correction fluid
el	**diccionario**	dictionary
el	**ejercicio**	exercise
el	**examinador**	examiner
el	**griego**	Greek
el	**jefe de estudios**	director of studies
el	**inspector**	school inspector
el	**internado**	boarding school
el	**interno**	boarder
el	**latín**	Latin
el	**libro de texto**	textbook
el	**maletín** (*pl* maletines)	briefcase
el	**parte (de faltas** *or* **ausencias)**	absence sheet
el	**parvulario**	nursery school
el	**profesor consejero**	form tutor
el	**pupitre**	desk
el	**rotulador**	felt-tip pen
el	**sacapuntas** (*pl inv*)	pencil sharpener
el	**test** (*pl* ~s)	test
el	**trabajo**	essay; class exam
el	**trimestre**	term
el	**vestuario**	cloakroom
el	**vocabulario**	vocabulary

USEFUL WORDS *(feminine)*

el	álgebra (f)	algebra
la	aritmética	arithmetic
la	bedel	janitor
la	calculadora	calculator
la	caligrafía	handwriting
la	carpintería	woodwork
la	cartera	satchel; schoolbag; briefcase
las	ciencias del medio ambiente	natural science
las	ciencias naturales	natural history
la	enseñanza religiosa	religious instruction
la	entrega de premios	prize-giving
la	ESO (Educación Secundaria Obligatoria) (Sp)	compulsory secondary education
la	facultad	faculty
la	fila	row (of seats etc)
la	FP (formación profesional) (Sp)	technical college
la	geometría	geometry
la	gramática	grammar
la	inspectora	school inspector
la	interna	boarder
la	mancha	blot
la	nota media	pass mark; average mark
la	ortografía	spelling
la	pizarra (electrónica) interactiva	interactive whiteboard
la	poesía	poetry; poem
la	prueba	test
las	TIC (tecnologías de la información y la comunicación)	ICT
la	tinta	ink
la	tiza	chalk
la	traducción inversa (pl traducciones ~s)	prose translation

ESSENTIAL WORDS (masculine)

el	aerogenerador	wind turbine
el	agujero	hole
el	aire	air
los	animales	animals
los	árboles	trees
el	bosque	wood
el	coche	car
el	diesel	diesel
el	ecologista	environmentalist
el	gas	gas
los	gases de escape	exhaust fumes
el	gasoil	diesel
los	habitantes	inhabitants
el	mapa	map
el	mar	sea
el	medio ambiente	environment
el	mundo	world
el	país	country
el	pescado	fish
el	tiempo	weather; time
los	Verdes	the Greens
el	vidrio	glass

IMPORTANT WORDS (masculine)

el	acontecimiento	event
el	aluminio	aluminium
el	calor	heat
el	clima	climate
el	contaminante	pollutant
el	daño	damage
el	detergente	detergent; washing powder
el	futuro	future
el	gobierno	government
el	impuesto	tax
el	lago	lake
el	parque eólico	windfarm
el	planeta	planet
el	río	river

ESSENTIAL WORDS *(feminine)*

el	agua *(f)*	water
las	botellas	bottles
la	contaminación	pollution
la	costa	coast
la	cuestión *(pl* cuestiones)	question
la	ecología	ecology
la	especie	species
la	fábrica	factory
la	flor	flower
la	fruta	fruit
la	gasolina	petrol
la	isla	island
la	lluvia	rain
la	montaña	mountain
la	planta	plant
la	playa	beach
la	región *(pl* regiones)	region; area
la	temperatura	temperature
la	tierra	earth
la(s)	verdura(s)	vegetables

IMPORTANT WORDS *(feminine)*

la	central nuclear	nuclear plant
la	crisis *(pl inv)*	crisis
la	legumbre	vegetable
la	selva	forest; jungle
la	solución *(pl* soluciones)	solution
la	zona	zone

USEFUL WORDS *(masculine)*

el	aerosol	aerosol
los	alimentos orgánicos	organic food
el	calentamiento global	global warming
el	canal	canal
el	catalizador	catalytic converter
el	CFC (clorofluorocarbono)	CFC
los	científicos	scientists
el	combustible	fuel
el	continente	continent
el	desarrollo sostenible	sustainable development
el	desierto	desert
el	ecosistema	ecosystem
el	fertilizante	(artificial) fertilizer
el	investigador	researcher
el	océano	ocean
el	OGM (organismo genéticamente modificado)	GMO
el	producto	product
los	productos químicos	chemicals
el	reciclado, el reciclaje	recycling
los	residuos nucleares/ industriales	nuclear/industrial waste
el	universo	universe
el	vertedero	dumping ground

USEFUL PHRASES

(él) es muy respetuoso con el medio ambiente **he's very environmentally-minded**

un producto ecológico **an eco-friendly product**

en el futuro **in the future**

destruir **to destroy**

contaminar **to contaminate; to pollute**

prohibir **to ban**

salvar **to save**

reciclar **to recycle**

verde **green**

USEFUL WORDS *(feminine)*

las	**aguas residuales**	sewage
la	**capa de ozono**	ozone layer
la	**catástrofe**	disaster
la	**contaminación acústica**	noise pollution
la	**energía eólica**	wind power
la	**energía nuclear**	nuclear power
la	**energía renovable**	renewable energy
la	**lluvia ácida**	acid rain
la	**luna**	moon
la	**marea negra**	oil slick
la	**población** (*pl* poblaciones)	population
la	**selva tropical**	tropical rainforest

USEFUL PHRASES

biodegradable **biodegradable**
nocivo(a) *or* dañino(a) para el medio ambiente **harmful to the environment**
orgánico(a), biológico(a), ecológico(a) **organic**
gasolina sin plomo **unleaded petrol**
(las) especies en peligro de extinción **endangered species**

ESSENTIAL WORDS (masculine)

el	**abuelo**	grandfather
los	**abuelos**	grandparents
los	**adultos**	adults
el	**apellido**	surname
el	**apellido de soltera**	maiden name
el	**bebé**	baby
la	**edad**	age
el	**hermano**	brother
el	**hijo**	son
el	**hombre**	man
el	**joven** (pl jóvenes)	youth, young man
los	**jóvenes**	young people
el	**marido**	husband
el	**niño**	child, boy
el	**nombre**	name
el	**nombre (de pila)**	first or Christian name
el	**novio**	fiancé
el	**padre**	father
los	**padres**	parents
el	**papá**	daddy
el	**pariente**	relative
el	**primo**	cousin
el	**prometido**	fiancé
el	**tío**	uncle

USEFUL PHRASES

¿qué edad tiene (or tienes)?, ¿cuántos años tiene (or tienes)? **how old are you?**

tengo 15 años – él tiene 40 años **I'm 15 – he is 40**

¿cómo se llama (or te llamas)? **what is your name?**

me llamo Daniela **my name is Daniela**

él se llama Paco **his name is Paco**

prometido(a) **engaged**

casado(a) **married**

divorciado(a) **divorced**

separado(a) **separated**

casarse con algn **to marry sb**

casarse **to get married**; divorciarse **to get divorced**

ESSENTIAL WORDS *(feminine)*

la	abuela	grandmother
la	familia	family
la	gente	people
la	hermana	sister
la	hija	daughter; girl
la	joven *(pl* jóvenes)	youth
la	madre	mother
la	mamá	mummy
los	mayores	grown-ups
la	mujer	woman; wife
la	niña	child, girl
la	novia	fiancée
la	persona	person
la	prima	cousin
la	prometida	fiancée
la	señora	lady
la	tía	aunt

USEFUL PHRASES

más joven/mayor que yo younger/older than me
¿tiene *(or* tienes) hermanos? do you have any brothers or sisters?
tengo un hermano y una hermana I have one brother and one sister
no tengo hermanos I don't have any brothers or sisters
soy hijo(a) único(a) I am an only child
toda la familia the whole family
crecer to grow
envejecer, hacerse viejo(a) to get old
me llevo bien con mis padres I get on well with my parents
mi madre trabaja my mother works

IMPORTANT WORDS (masculine)

el	adolescente	teenager
el	esposo	husband
el	nieto	grandson
los	nietos	grandchildren
el	padrastro	stepfather
el	sobrino	nephew
el	soltero	bachelor
el	subsidio familiar (por hijos)	child benefit
el	suegro	father-in-law
el	vecino	neighbour
el	viudo	widower

USEFUL WORDS (masculine)

el	ahijado	godson
el	anciano	old man
el	apodo	nickname
el	chaval, el chico	kid
el	cuñado	brother-in-law
los	gemelos	identical twins
el	hermanastro	stepbrother
el	hijastro	stepson
el	huérfano	orphan
el	jubilado	pensioner
el	marido	bridegroom
los	mellizos	twins
el	mote	nickname
el	padrino	godfather
los	recién casados	newlyweds
los	trillizos	triplets
el	viejo	old man
el	yerno	son-in-law

USEFUL PHRASES

nacer to be born; vivir to live; morir to die
nací en 1990 I was born in 1990
mi abuela murió or está muerta my grandmother is dead
ella murió en 1995 she died in 1995

IMPORTANT WORDS *(feminine)*

la	**adolescente**	teenager
la	**au pair** *(pl inv)*	au pair girl
la	**esposa**	wife
la	**madrastra**	stepmother
la	**nieta**	granddaughter
la	**sobrina**	niece
la	**soltera**	single woman
la	**suegra**	mother-in-law
la	**vecina**	neighbour
la	**viuda**	widow

USEFUL WORDS *(feminine)*

la	**ahijada**	goddaughter
el	**ama de casa** *(pl f* las amas ~~)	housewife
la	**anciana**	old woman
la	**chavala,** la **chica**	kid
la	**cuñada**	sister-in-law
las	**gemelas**	identical twins
la	**hermanastra**	stepsister
la	**hijastra**	stepdaughter
la	**huérfana**	orphan
la	**jubilada**	pensioner
la	**madrina**	godmother
las	**mellizas**	twins, twin sisters
la	**niñera**	nanny
la	**novia**	bride
la	**nuera**	daughter-in-law
la	**pareja**	couple
la	**vejez**	old age
la	**vieja**	old woman

USEFUL PHRASES

él/ella es soltero(a) he/she is single
él es viudo he is a widower; ella es viuda she is a widow
soy el/la más joven I am the youngest; soy el/la mayor I am the eldest
mi hermana mayor my older sister

ESSENTIAL WORDS *(masculine)*

el	agricultor *(Sp)*	farmer
el	animal	animal
el	bosque	forest
el	buey	ox
el	caballo	horse
el	cabrito	kid
el	campo	field; country
el	cerdo	pig
el	chivo	kid
el	gato	cat
el	granjero	farmer
el	invernadero	greenhouse
el	pato	duck
el	pavo	turkey
el	perro	dog
el	perro pastor *(pl ~s ~)*	sheepdog
el	pollo	chicken
el	pueblo	village
el	ranchero *(Mex)*	farmer
el	ternero	calf

IMPORTANT WORDS *(masculine)*

el	campesino	countryman
el	cordero	lamb
el	gallo	cock
el	tractor	tractor

USEFUL PHRASES

un trigal, un maizal a cornfield
la agricultura ecológica organic farming
los pollos de granja free range chickens
los huevos de corral free range eggs
cuidar los animales to look after the animals
recolectar to harvest
recoger la cosecha to bring in the harvest/crops

ESSENTIAL WORDS *(feminine)*

la	**agricultora** *(Sp)*	farmer
la	**camioneta** *(Sp)*	van
la	**cerda**	sow
la	**finca**	farm
la	**gallina**	hen
la	**granja**	farm; farmhouse
la	**granjera**	farmer; farmer's wife
la	**oveja**	sheep; ewe
la	**puerta**	gate
la	**ranchera** *(Mex)*	farmer
la	**tierra**	earth; ground
la	**vaca**	cow
la	**vagoneta** *(Mex)*	van
la	**valla**	fence
la	**verja**	gate
la	**yegua**	mare

IMPORTANT WORDS *(feminine)*

la	**campesina**	countrywoman
la	**colina**	hill

USEFUL PHRASES

vivir en el campo to live in the country
trabajar en una granja to work on a farm
recolectar el heno to make hay

USEFUL WORDS *(masculine)*

el	abono	manure; fertilizer
el	almiar	haystack
el	arado	plough
el	barro	mud
el	burro	donkey
el	carnero	ram
el	centeno	rye
el	cerdo	pig
el	cereal	cereal, crop
el	cobertizo	shed
el	corral	farmyard
el	espantapájaros *(pl inv)*	scarecrow
el	establo	cow shed, byre
el	estanque	pond
el	estiércol	manure
el	gallinero	henhouse
el	ganado	cattle
el	ganso	goose
el	granero	barn
el	grano	grain, seed
el	heno	hay
el	maíz *(pl* maices*)*	maize
el	molino *(de viento)*	(wind)mill
el	paisaje	landscape
el	pajar	loft
el	páramo	moor, heath
el	pastor	shepherd
el	pollito	chick
el	potro	foal
el	pozo	well
el	prado	meadow
el	rebaño	*(sheep)* flock; *(cattle)* herd
el	suelo	ground, earth
el	surco	furrow
el	toro	bull
el	trigo	corn; wheat

USEFUL WORDS *(feminine)*

la	avena	oats
la	cabra	goat
la	cabritilla	kid
la	carretilla	cart
la	casita (con el tejado de paja)	(thatched) cottage
la	cebada	barley
la	cosecha	crop
la	cosechadora	combine harvester
la	cuadra	stable
la	escalera	ladder
la	ganadería	cattle farm
la	lana	wool
la	lonja	market
la	paja	straw
la	pocilga	pigsty
la	recolección *(pl* recolecciones)	harvest
la	uva	grapes
la	vendimia	grape harvest, grape picking
la	viña	vine
la	zanja	ditch

ESSENTIAL WORDS (masculine)

el	marisco	seafood
el	pez (pl peces)	fish
el	pez de colores (pl peces ~ ~)	goldfish

IMPORTANT WORDS (masculine)

| el | cangrejo | crab |
| el | insecto | insect |

USEFUL WORDS (masculine)

el	acuario	aquarium
el	arenque	herring
el	atún (pl atunes)	tuna
el	avispón (pl avispones)	hornet
el	bacalao	cod
el	calamar	squid
el	camarón (pl camarones)	shrimp
el	cangrejo de río	crayfish
el	chinche	bug
el	eglefino	haddock
el	grillo	cricket
el	gusano	worm
el	gusano de seda	silkworm
los	langostinos	scampi
el	lenguado	sole
el	lucio	pike
el	mejillón (pl mejillones)	mussel
el	mosquito	mosquito
el	pulpo	octopus
el	renacuajo	tadpole
el	salmón (pl salmones)	salmon
el	saltamontes (pl inv)	grasshopper
el	tiburón (pl tiburones)	shark

USEFUL PHRASES

nadar to swim
volar to fly
vamos a ir a pescar we're going fishing

ESSENTIAL WORDS *(feminine)*

el   agua *(f)*   water

IMPORTANT WORDS *(feminine)*

la   mosca   fly
la   sardina   sardine
la   trucha   trout

USEFUL WORDS *(feminine)*

la   abeja   bee
el   ala *(pl f* las alas)   wing
la   anguila   eel
la   araña   spider
la   avispa   wasp
la   cigala   crayfish
la   cigarra   cicada
la   cucaracha   cockroach
la   hormiga   ant
la   langosta   lobster
la   libélula   dragonfly
la   mariposa   butterfly
la   mariquita   ladybird
la   medusa   jellyfish
la   mosquilla   midge
la   mosquita   midge
la   oruga   caterpillar
la   ostra   oyster
la   pescadilla   whiting
la   polilla   moth
la   pulga   flea
la   rana   frog

USEFUL PHRASES

una picadura de avispa a wasp sting
una tela de araña a spider's web

ESSENTIAL WORDS (*masculine*)

el	**aceite**	oil
el	**agua mineral**	(mineral) water
el	**alcohol**	alcohol
el	**almuerzo**	lunch
el	**aperitivo**	aperitif
el	**arroz**	rice
el	**asado**	roast
el	**autoservicio**	self-service restaurant
el	**azúcar**	sugar
el	**bar**	bar
el	**bistec** (*pl inv or* ~s)	steak
el	**bol**	bowl
el	**bote**	tin, can
el	**café**	coffee; café
el	**café con leche**	coffee with milk
el	**café con más leche**	milky coffee
el	**camarero** (*Sp*)	waiter
los	**caramelos**	sweets
el	**cerdo**	pork
los	**cereales**	cereal
el	**chocolate (caliente)**	(hot) chocolate
el	**cocinero**	cook
el	**consomé**	soup
el	**croissant** *or* el **cruasán** (*pl* cruasanes)	croissant
el	**cuarto**	quarter (*bottle/litre etc*)
el	**cuenco**	bowl
el	**cuchillo**	knife
el	**desayuno**	breakfast
el	**dueño**	owner
los	**entrantes**	hors d'œuvres, starters
el	**entrecot** (*pl inv or* ~s)	(entrecôte) steak
el	**filete**	steak
el	**helado**	ice cream
el	**huevo**	egg
el	**huevo duro** *or* **cocido**	hard-boiled egg
el	**huevo pasado por agua**	soft-boiled egg
el	**jamón** (*pl* jamones)	ham

ESSENTIAL WORDS *(feminine)*

la	aceituna	olive
la	baguette *(pl inv or ~s)*	French loaf
la	bandeja	tray
la	bebida	drink
la	botella	bottle
la	caja	box
la	carne	meat
la	carne de vaca	beef
la	carta	menu
la	cena	dinner
la	cerveza	beer
la	Coca-Cola® *(pl ~s)*	Coke®
la	comida	lunch; meal
la	comida precocinada *or* preparada	ready-made meal
las	conservas	canned food
la	cuchara	spoon
la	cuenta	bill
la	ensalada	salad
la	ensalada mixta	mixed salad
la	fruta	fruit
el	hambre *(f)*	hunger
la	hamburguesa	hamburger
la	lata	tin, can
la	leche	milk
la	limonada	lemonade
la	loncha (de)	slice (of)
la	mantequilla	butter
la	mermelada	jam
la	mermelada (de cítricos)	marmalade
la	mesa	table
la	pastelería	pastry; cake shop
las	patatas fritas	chips; crisps
la	pescadería	fish shop
la	pieza de fruta	piece of fruit
la	repostería	pastry; cake shop
la	sal	salt
la	salchicha	sausage

ESSENTIAL WORDS (masculine continued)

el	marisco	seafood
el	menú del día	fixed-price menu
el	mesero (LAm)	waiter
el	pan	bread
el	paté	pâté
el	pescado	fish
el	picnic (pl inv or ~s)	picnic
el	platillo	saucer
el	plato	plate; dish; course
el	plato del día	today's special
el	pollo (asado)	(roast) chicken
el	postre	dessert
el	primero, el primer plato	first course, starter
el	queso	cheese
el	quiche (pl inv)	quiche
el	restaurante	restaurant
el	salami, el salchichón (pl salchichones)	salami
el	sándwich (pl ~s or ~es)	sandwich
el	self-service (pl inv)	self-service restaurant
el	servicio	service
el	té	tea
el	tenedor	fork
el	vaso	glass
el	vinagre	vinegar
el	vino	wine
el	yogur(t)	yoghurt
el	zumo de fruta	fruit juice

USEFUL PHRASES

cocinar to cook; comer to eat
beber to drink; tragar to swallow
mi plato favorito my favourite dish
¿qué vas (or va) a beber? what are you having to drink?
está bueno or rico it's nice
estar hambriento, tener hambre to be hungry
estar sediendo, tener sed to be thirsty

ESSENTIAL WORDS *(feminine continued)*

la	sed *(pl inv)*	thirst
la	sidra	cider
la	sopa	soup
la	tarta	cake
la	taza	cup
la	ternera	veal
la	tortilla francesa	omelette
la	tortita	pancake
la	tostada	toast
la	vajilla	dishes
las	verduras	vegetables

IMPORTANT WORDS *(feminine)*

la	cafetería	cafeteria
la	camarera	waitress
la	carne asada *or* a la parrilla	grilled meat
la	cerveza de barril	draught beer
la	chef *(pl inv or ~s)*	chef
la	chuleta de cerdo	pork chop
la	cucharilla	teaspoon
la	cucharita (de postre)	dessertspoon
la	cuchara de servir	tablespoon
la	garrafa	carafe
la	harina	flour
la	jarra	jug
la	mayonesa	mayonnaise
la	mostaza	mustard
la	nata	cream
las	patatas fritas (de bolsa)	crisps
la	pimienta	pepper
la	pizza	pizza
la	propina	tip
la	receta	recipe
la	selección *(pl* selecciones*)*	choice
la	tarta	tart
la	tetera	teapot
la	vainilla	vanilla

IMPORTANT WORDS (*masculine*)

el	ajo	garlic
el	almíbar	syrup
el	aperitivo	snack
el	camarero	waiter
los	caracoles	snails
el	carrito	trolley
el	chef (*pl inv or* ~s)	chef
el	cocinero jefe	chef
el	conejo	rabbit
el	cordero	lamb; mutton
el	cubierto	cover charge; place setting
el	gusto	taste
el	olor	smell
el	precio con todo incluido	inclusive price
el	precio fijo	set price
el	refresco concentrado	cordial
el	restaurante	restaurant
el	sabor	flavour
el	suplemento	extra charge
el	tentempié	snack

USEFUL WORDS (*masculine*)

el	abrelatas (*pl inv*)	tin opener
el	aperitivo	snack
el	beicon	bacon
el	biscote	Melba toast
el	bollito	roll
el	bollo	bun
el	cacao	cocoa
el	coñac (*pl inv*)	brandy
el	corcho	cork
el	cubito (de hielo)	ice cube
el	champán (*pl* champanes)	champagne
el	estofado	stew
el	foie gras (*pl inv*)	liver pâté
el	hígado	liver
el	ketchup (*pl inv*)	ketchup
el	mantel	tablecloth

USEFUL WORDS *(feminine)*

las	**aves**	poultry
la	**carta de vinos**	wine list
la	**caza**	game
la	**chuleta**	chop
la	**clara**	shandy
la	**comida**	food
la	**gelatina**	jelly
la	**infusión** (*pl* infusiones)	herbal tea
la	**jarra**	jug
la	**margarina**	margarine
la	**miel**	honey
la	**miga**	crumb
la	**nata montada**	whipped cream
las	**natillas**	custard
la	**pajita**	straw
la	**pasta**	pasta
la	**rebanada**	piece of bread and butter
la	**salsa**	sauce
la	**salsa de jugo de carne**	gravy
la	**servilleta**	napkin
la	**tisana**	herbal tea
las	**tripas**	tripe
la	**tostada**	slice of toast
la	**vinagreta**	vinaigrette dressing

USEFUL PHRASES

fregar los platos to do the dishes
cuando volvemos del colegio merendamos we have a snack when we
  come back from school
desayunar, tomar el desayuno to have breakfast
delicioso(a) delicious; repugnante disgusting
¡que aproveche! enjoy your meal!; ¡salud! cheers!
¡la cuenta, por favor! the bill please!
"servicio (no) incluido" "service (not) included"
comer fuera to eat out
invitar a algn a comer to invite sb to lunch
tomar algo de beber, beber algo to have drinks

USEFUL WORDS *(masculine continued)*

los	mejillones	mussels
el	panecillo	roll
el	paté de carne	potted meat
el	paté de hígado	liver pâté
el	paté de oca	goose pâté
el	puré de patatas	mashed potatoes
los	riñones	kidneys
el	rosbif *(pl inv or ~s)*	roast beef
el	sacacorchos *(pl inv)*	corkscrew
el	tapón *(pl tapones)*	cork
el	termo	flask
el	torrezno	diced bacon
el	whisky, whiskey *(pl ~s)*	whisky
el	zumo natural de limón	freshly-squeezed lemon juice

USEFUL PHRASES

poner la mesa to set the table; quitar la mesa to clear the table
comer, almorzar to have lunch
cenar to have dinner
probar algo to taste sth
¡eso huele bien! that smells good!
vino blanco/rosado/tinto white/rosé/red wine
un filete poco hecho/en su punto/bien hecho a rare/medium/
   well-done steak
un sándwich (tostado) de jamón y queso a ham and cheese toastie

SMOKING

el	**cenicero**	ashtray
la	**cerilla**	match
el	**cigarrillo**	cigarette
el	**cigarro**	cigar
el	**estanco**	tobacconist's
el	**mechero**	lighter
la	**pipa**	pipe
el	**tabaco**	tobacco

USEFUL PHRASES

una caja de cerillas a box of matches
¿tienes (or tiene) fuego? do you have a light?
encender un cigarrillo to light up
"prohibido fumar" "no smoking"
no fumo I don't smoke
he dejado de fumar, he dejado el tabaco I've stopped smoking
fumar es perjudicial para tu or la salud smoking is very bad for you

ESSENTIAL WORDS (*masculine*)

el	**ajedrez**	chess
el	**amigo por correspondencia**	pen friend
el	**baile**	dance
el	**billete** (*Sp*)	ticket
el	**boleto** (*LAm*)	ticket
el	**cantante**	singer
el	**canto**	singing
el	**CD** (*pl inv or* ~s)	CD
el	**cine**	cinema
el	**club** (*pl* ~s *or* ~es)	club
el	**concierto**	concert
los	**deportes**	sports
el	**dinero de bolsillo**	pocket money
el	**disco**	record
el	**DVD** (*pl inv or* ~s)	DVD
el	**espectáculo**	show
el	**fin de semana**	weekend
el	**folleto**	leaflet
el	**futbolín** (*pl* futbolines)	table football
el	**hobby** (*pl* hobbies)	hobby
el	**Internet**	internet
el	**juego**	game
el	**lector de CD/DVD/MP3**	CD/DVD/MP3 player
el	**miembro**	member
el	**museo**	museum; art gallery
el	**paseo**	walk
el	**periódico**	newspaper
el	**programa**	programme
el	**teatro**	theatre
el	**(teléfono) móvil** (*Sp*) *or* **celular** (*LAm*)	mobile (phone)
el	**tiempo libre**	free time
el	**videojuego**	video game
el	**walkman**® (*pl* ~s)	personal stereo

ESSENTIAL WORDS *(feminine)*

la	**afición** *(pl* aficiones)	hobby
la	**amiga por correspondencia**	pen friend
la	**cadena de televisión**	TV channel
la	**cámara (de fotos)**	camera
la	**canción** *(pl* canciones)	song
la	**cantante**	singer
las	**cartas**	cards
la	**disco(teca)**	disco
la	**diversión** *(pl* diversiones)	entertainment
la	**estrella (de cine)** *(m+f)*	(film) star
la	**excursión** *(pl* excursiones)	trip; outing; hike
la	**fiesta**	party
la	**foto**	photo
la	**historieta**	comic strip
la	**lectura**	reading
la	**música (pop/clásica)**	(pop/classical) music
las	**noticias**	news
la	**novela**	novel
la	**novela policíaca** *or* **policiaca**	detective novel
la	**película**	film
la	**pista de patinaje**	skating rink
la	**prensa**	the press
la	**publicidad**	publicity
la	**radio**	radio
la	**revista**	magazine
la	**tele(visión)** *(pl* teles, televisiones)	television, TV
la	**videoconsola**	games console

USEFUL PHRASES

salgo con mis amigos I go out with my friends
leo el periódico I read the newspaper
veo la televisión I watch television
juego al fútbol/al tenis/a las cartas I play football/tennis/cards
hacer bricolaje to do DIY
hacer de canguro to baby-sit
hacer zapping to channel-hop
ir de discoteca *or* marcha *(Sp)* to go clubbing

IMPORTANT WORDS *(masculine)*

el	**anuncio**	notice; poster
los	**anuncios por palabras**	adverts; small ads
el	**carrete**	film (*for camera*)
el	**compact disc** (*pl ~ ~s*)	compact disc, CD
el	**concurso**	competition
los	**dibujos animados**	cartoon
el	**juguete**	toy
el	**mensaje de texto**	text message
el	**noticiero** (*LAm*)	news
el	**novio**	boyfriend
el	**ordenador (personal)** (*Sp*)	personal computer
los	**pasatiempos**	leisure activities
el	**PC** (*pl inv*)	PC
el	**programa**	programme
el	**punto**	knitting
el	**SMS** (*pl inv*)	text message
el	**telediario** (*Sp*)	news
el	**vídeo** (*Sp*), el **video** (*LAm*)	video recorder
el	**website**	website

USEFUL WORDS *(masculine)*

el	**aficionado**	fan
el	**blog**	blog
el	**campamento de verano**	holiday camp
el	**chat**	chat; chatroom
el	**club nocturno** (*pl ~s or ~es ~s*)	night club
el	**coro**	choir
el	**crucigrama**	crossword puzzle(s)
el	**explorador**	scout
el	**juego de mesa**	board game
el	**monopatín** (*pl* monopatines)	skateboard
el	**videoclub** (*pl ~s or ~es*)	video shop

USEFUL PHRASES

emocionante exciting
aburrido(a) boring
divertido(a) funny

IMPORTANT WORDS *(feminine)*

la	**cámara digital**	digital camera
la	**casa de la juventud**	youth club
la	**cinta**	tape
la	**cinta de vídeo**	video cassette
la	**colección** (*pl* colecciones)	collection
la	**computadora (personal)** (*LAm*)	personal computer
la	**exposición** (*pl* exposiciones)	exhibition
la	**filmadora** (*LAm*)	camcorder
la	**grabadora de CD/DVD**	CD/DVD writer
la	**noche**	evening
la	**novia**	girlfriend
la	**pintura**	painting
la	**reunión** (*pl* reuniones)	meeting
la	**serie**	serial
la	**tarde**	evening
la	**telenovela**	soap (opera)
la	**videocámara** (*Sp*)	camcorder

USEFUL WORDS *(feminine)*

la	**aficionada**	fan
la	**diapositiva**	slide
la	**exploradora**	(girl) guide, girl scout
la	**fotografía**	photograph; photography
la	**lista de éxitos**	charts

USEFUL PHRASES

no está mal it's not bad
bastante bien quite good
bailar to dance
hacer fotos to take photos
estoy aburrido(a) I'm bored
quedamos los viernes we meet on Fridays
estoy ahorrando para comprarme un DVD I'm saving up to buy a DVD
me gustaría dar la vuelta al mundo I'd like to go round the world

ESSENTIAL WORDS *(masculine)*

el **albaricoque**	apricot
el **limón** *(pl* limones)	lemon
el **melocotón** *(pl* melocotones)	peach
el **plátano**	banana
el **pomelo**	grapefruit
el **tomate**	tomato

IMPORTANT WORDS *(masculine)*

el **árbol frutal**	fruit tree
el **melón** *(pl* melones)	melon

USEFUL WORDS *(masculine)*

el **aguacate**	avocado
el **anacardo**	cashew nut
el **arándano**	blueberry
el **cacahuete**	peanut
el **coco**	coconut
el **dátil**	date
el **higo**	fig
el **hueso**	stone *(in fruit)*
el **kiwi**	kiwi fruit
el **ruibarbo**	rhubarb

ESSENTIAL WORDS *(feminine)*

la	**castaña (asada)**	(roasted) chestnut
la	**cereza**	cherry
la	**frambuesa**	raspberry
la	**fresa**	strawberry
la	**fruta**	fruit
la	**manzana**	apple
la	**naranja**	orange
la	**pasa**	raisin
la	**pera**	pear
la	**piel**	skin
la	**(pieza de) fruta**	(piece of) fruit
la	**piña**	pineapple
la	**uva**	grape(s)

USEFUL WORDS *(feminine)*

la	**avellana**	hazelnut
la	**baya**	berry
la	**ciruela**	plum
la	**ciruela pasa**	prune
la	**granada**	pomegranate
la	**grosella espinosa**	gooseberry
la	**grosella negra**	blackcurrant
la	**grosella (roja)**	redcurrant
la	**mandarina**	tangerine
la	**mora**	blackberry
la	**nuez** *(pl* nueces)	nut; walnut
la	**pepita**	pip *(in fruit)*
la	**vid**	vine

USEFUL PHRASES

un zumo de naranja/piña an orange/a pineapple juice
un racimo de uvas a bunch of grapes
maduro(a) ripe
verde unripe
pelar una fruta to peel a fruit
resbalar al pisar una cáscara de plátano to slip on a banana skin

ESSENTIAL WORDS (masculine)

el	**armario** (*Sp*)	cupboard; wardrobe
el	**calefactor**	heater
el	**congelador**	freezer
el	**equipo** (de música)	stereo system
el	**espejo**	mirror
el	**frigo**	fridge
el	**frigorífico** (*Sp*)	fridge
el	**mueble**	piece of furniture
los	**muebles**	furniture
el	**radiodespertador**	radio alarm
el	**refrigerador** (*LAm*)	fridge
el	**reloj**	clock
el	**ropero** (*LAm*)	cupboard; wardrobe
el	**sillón** (*pl* sillones)	armchair
el	**teléfono**	telephone
el	**transistor**	transistor

IMPORTANT WORDS (masculine)

el	**aparador**	sideboard
el	**aparato**	appliance
el	**casete**	tape recorder
el	**cuadro**	picture
el	**escritorio**	(writing) desk
el	**hervidor**	kettle
el	**horno microondas**	microwave oven
el	**inalámbrico**	cordless phone
el	**lavavajillas** (*pl inv*)	dishwasher
el	**lector de CD/DVD**	CD/DVD player
el	**piano**	piano
el	**portátil**	laptop
el	**sofá**	sofa
el	**(teléfono) móvil** (*Sp*) or **celular** (*LAm*)	mobile phone
el	**vídeo** (*Sp*), el **video** (*LAm*)	video recorder

ESSENTIAL WORDS *(feminine)*

la	**balda**	shelf
la	**cama**	bed
la	**cocina (eléctrica/de gas)**	(electric/gas) cooker
la	**estufa**	heater
la	**habitación** (*pl* habitaciones)	room
la	**lámpara**	lamp
la	**lavadora**	washing machine
la	**mesa**	table
la	**pantalla (de lámpara)**	lampshade
la	**radio**	radio
la	**silla**	chair
la	**televisión** (*pl* televisiones)	television

IMPORTANT WORDS *(feminine)*

el	**arca** (*f pl* las arcas)	chest
la	**aspiradora**	vacuum cleaner
la	**librería**	bookcase
la	**mesa de centro**	coffee table
la	**pintura**	painting
la	**plancha**	iron
la	**radio digital**	digital radio
la	**secadora**	tumble-dryer

USEFUL WORDS (*masculine*)

la	**altavoz** (*pl* altavoces)	loudspeaker
el	**asiento**	seat
el	**cajón** (*pl* cajones)	drawer
el	**camión de mudanzas** (*pl* camiones ~~)	removal van
el	**carrito**	trolley
el	**colchón** (*pl* colchones)	mattress
el	**contestador**	answering machine
el	**horno**	oven
el	**mando a distancia**	remote control
el	**marco**	frame
el	**mobiliario**	furniture
el	**operario de mudanzas**	removal man
el	**paragüero**	umbrella stand
el	**peso**	scales
los	**postigos**	shutters
el	**robot de cocina** (*pl* ~ s ~~)	food processor
el	**secador (de pelo)**	hairdryer
el	**taburete**	stool
el	**teléfono inalámbrico**	cordless telephone
el	**tocador**	dressing table

USEFUL PHRASES

un apartamento *or* piso amueblado a furnished flat
encender/apagar el calefactor *or* la estufa to switch the heater on/off
he hecho la cama I've made my bed
sentarse to sit down
poner *or* meter algo en el horno to put sth in the oven
correr las cortinas to draw the curtains
cerrar los postigos *or* las contraventanas to close the shutters

USEFUL WORDS *(feminine)*

la	**alfombra**	rug
la	**antena**	aerial
la	**antena parabólica**	satellite dish
la	**cadena de música**	music centre
la	**cámara cinematográfica**	cine camera
la	**cómoda**	chest of drawers
las	**contraventanas**	shutters
la	**cuna**	cradle; cot
la	**estantería**	shelves
la	**lámpara de pie**	standard lamp
la	**lámpara halógena**	halogen lamp
las	**literas**	bunk beds
la	**máquina de coser**	sewing machine
la	**máquina de escribir**	typewriter
la	**mesilla de noche**	bedside table
la	**moqueta**	fitted carpet
la	**mudanza**	move
la	**persiana**	blind
la	**tabla de planchar**	ironing board
la	**videocámara**	video camera, camcorder

USEFUL PHRASES

es un piso de 4 habitaciones **it's a 4-roomed flat**

¡ya está el desayuno/la comida/la cena! **breakfast/lunch/dinner is ready!**

ESSENTIAL WORDS

los	Alpes	the Alps
	Andalucía	Andalusia
el	Atlántico	the Atlantic
	Barcelona	Barcelona
	Bruselas	Brussels
	Castilla	Castile
	Cataluña	Catalonia
la	Costa del Sol	the Costa del Sol
el	este	the east
las	Islas Baleares	the Balearic Islands
las	Islas Canarias	the Canary Islands
la	Coruña	Corunna
	Londres	London
	Málaga	Malaga
	Mallorca	Majorca
el	Mar Cantábrico	the Bay of Biscay
el	Mediterráneo	the Mediterranean
	Menorca	Minorca
el	norte	the north
el	oeste	the west
el	País Vasco	the Basque Country
el	Peñón (de Gibraltar)	the Rock (of Gibraltar)
los	Pirineos	the Pyrenees
	Sevilla	Seville
la	sierra	mountain range
el	sur	the south
	Vizcaya	Biscay
	Zaragoza	Saragossa

IMPORTANT WORDS

	Edimburgo	Edinburgh
el	Támesis	the Thames

USEFUL WORDS

	Atenas	Athens
	Berlín	Berlin
la	capital	capital
la	comunidad autónoma	autonomous region (*of Spain*)
el	Extremo Oriente	the Far East
	Ginebra	Geneva
las	Islas Británicas	the British Isles
la	Haya	The Hague
	Lisboa	Lisbon
	Marruecos	Morocco
	Moscú	Moscow
el	Oriente Medio	the Middle East
el	Oriente Próximo	the Near East
el	Pacífico	the Pacific
	París	Paris
	Pekín	Beijing
el	Polo Norte/Sur	the North/South Pole
la	provincia	province
	Roma	Rome
	Varsovia	Warsaw
	Venecia	Venice
	Viena	Vienna

USEFUL PHRASES

ir a Londres/Sevilla to go to London/Seville
ir a Andalucía to go to Andalusia
vengo de Barcelona/del País Vasco I come from Barcelona/the Basque Country

en el *or* al norte in *or* to the north
en el *or* al sur in *or* to the south
en el *or* al este in *or* to the east
en el *or* al oeste in *or* to the west

GREETINGS

hola hello
¿cómo está usted (*or* estás)? how are you?
¿qué tal? how are you?
bien fine (*in reply*)
encantado(a) pleased to meet you
¿dígame? hello (*on telephone*)
buenas tardes good afternoon; good evening
buenas noches good evening; good night
adiós goodbye; hello (*when passing one another*)
hasta mañana see you tomorrow
hasta luego see you later

BEST WISHES

feliz cumpleaños happy birthday
feliz Navidad merry Christmas
feliz Año Nuevo happy New Year
felices Pascuas happy Easter
recuerdos best wishes
saludos best wishes
bienvenido(a) welcome
enhorabuena congratulations
que aproveche enjoy your meal
que le vaya (*or* te vaya) bien all the best
que te diviertas (*or* se divierta) enjoy yourself
buena suerte good luck
buen viaje safe journey
jesús bless you (*after a sneeze*)
salud cheers
a tu (*or* vuestra, *etc*) salud good health

SURPRISE

Dios mío my goodness
¿qué?, ¿cómo? what?
entiendo oh, I see
vaya well, well
pues... well...
(¿)de verdad(?), (¿)sí(?) really(?)
(¿)estás (or está) de broma(?) you're kidding; are you kidding?
¡qué suerte! how lucky!

POLITENESS

perdone I'm sorry; excuse me
por favor please
gracias thank you
no, gracias no thank you
sí, gracias yes please
de nada not at all, don't mention it, you're welcome
con mucho gusto gladly

AGREEMENT

sí yes
por supuesto of course
de acuerdo, vale (*Sp*) OK
bueno fine

DISAGREEMENT

no no
que no no (*contradicting a positive statement*)
que sí yes (*contradicting a negative statement*)
claro que no of course not
ni hablar no way
en absoluto not at all
al contrario on the contrary
no me digas well I never
qué cara what a cheek
no te metas en lo que no te importa mind your own business

DIFFICULTIES

socorro help
fuego fire
ay ouch
perdón (I'm) sorry, excuse me, I beg your pardon
lo siento I'm sorry
qué pena what a pity
qué pesadez, qué rollo what a nuisance; how boring
estoy harto(a) I'm fed up
no aguanto más I can't stand it any more
vaya (por Dios) oh dear
qué horror how awful

ORDERS

cuidado be careful
para (*or* **pare**) stop
oiga, usted hey, you there
fuera de aquí clear off
silencio shh
basta ya that's enough
prohibido fumar no smoking
vamos, venga come on, let's go
sigue go ahead, go on
vámonos let's go

OTHERS

no tengo (ni) idea no idea
quizá, quizás perhaps, maybe
no (lo) sé I don't know
¿qué desea? can I help you?
aquí tienes there, there you are
ya voy just coming
no te preocupes don't worry
no merece la pena it's not worth it
a propósito by the way
cariño, querido(a) darling
el (*or* **la**) **pobre** poor thing
tanto mejor so much the better
no me importa I don't mind
a mí me da igual it's all the same to me
mala suerte too bad
depende it depends
¿qué voy a hacer? what shall I do?
¿para qué? what's the point?
me molesta it annoys me
me saca de quicio it gets on my nerves

ESSENTIAL WORDS (*masculine*)

el	**accidente**	accident
el	**dentista**	dentist
el	**doctor**	doctor
el	**enfermero**	(male) nurse
el	**enfermo**	patient
el	**estómago**	stomach
el	**hospital**	hospital
el	**médico**	doctor

IMPORTANT WORDS (*masculine*)

el	**algodón (hidrófilo)**	cotton wool
el	**antiséptico**	antiseptic
el	**comprimido**	tablet
el	**dolor**	pain
el	**esparadrapo**	(sticking) plaster
el	**farmacéutico**	chemist
el	**jarabe**	syrup
el	**medicamento**	medicine, drug
el	**paciente**	patient
el	**resfriado**	cold
el	**seguro**	insurance

USEFUL PHRASES

ha habido un accidente there's been an accident
ingresar en el hospital to be admitted to hospital
debe permanecer en cama you must stay in bed
estar enfermo(a) to be ill; sentirse mejor to feel better
cuidar to look after
me he hecho daño I have hurt myself
me he hecho un corte en el dedo I have cut my finger
me he torcido el tobillo I have sprained my ankle
se ha roto el brazo he has broken his arm
me he quemado I have burnt myself
me duele la garganta/la cabeza/ el estómago I've got a sore throat/
   a headache/a stomach ache
tener fiebre to have a temperature

ESSENTIAL WORDS *(feminine)*

la	aspirina	aspirin
la	cama	bed
la	cita	appointment
la	dentista	dentist
la	doctora	doctor
la	enferma	patient
la	enfermera	nurse
la	farmacia	chemist's *(shop)*
la	médico	doctor
la	pastilla	tablet, pill
la	salud	health
la	temperatura	temperature

IMPORTANT WORDS *(feminine)*

la	ambulancia	ambulance
la	camilla	stretcher
la	clínica	clinic, private hospital
la	consulta	surgery
la	crema	cream, ointment
la	cucharada	spoonful
la	diarrea	diarrhoea
la	enfermedad	illness
la	escayola	plaster cast
la	farmacéutica	chemist
la	gripe	flu
la	herida	wound, injury
la	insolación *(pl* insolaciones*)*	sunstroke
la	inyección *(pl* inyecciones*)*	injection
la	medicina	medicine
la	operación *(pl* operaciones*)*	operation
la	paciente	patient
la	píldora	pill; the Pill
las	quemaduras del sol	sunburn
la	receta	prescription
la	sangre	blood
la	tableta	tablet
las	urgencias	Accident and Emergency
la	venda	bandage

USEFUL WORDS *(masculine)*

el	absceso	abscess
el	acné	acne
el	arañazo	scratch
el	ataque	fit
el	ataque al corazón	heart attack
el	cáncer	cancer
el	cardenal	bruise
el	embarazo	pregnancy
el	estrés	stress
el	mareo	dizzy spell; sickness
el	microbio	germ
el	nervio	nerve
el	preservativo	condom
los	primeros auxilios	first aid
el	pulso	pulse
el	régimen	diet
el	reposo	rest
el	SAMU	emergency medical service
el	sarampión	measles
el	shock	shock
el	sida	AIDS
el	tónico	tonic
el	vendaje	dressing
el	veneno	poison

USEFUL PHRASES

tengo sueño I'm sleepy
tengo naúseas I feel sick
adelgazar to lose weight
engordar to put on weight
tragar to swallow
sangrar to bleed
vomitar to vomit
estar en forma to be in good shape
reposar, descansar to rest

USEFUL WORDS (*feminine*)

la	amigdalitis	tonsillitis
las	anginas	sore throat; tonsillitis
la	apendicitis	appendicitis
la	astilla	splinter
la	cicatriz (*pl* cicatrices)	scar
la	dentadura postiza	false teeth
la	dieta	diet
la	epidemia	epidemic
la	fiebre del heno	hay fever
la	migraña	migraine
la	muleta	crutch
la	náusea	nausea
las	paperas	mumps
la	pomada	ointment
la	radiografía	X-ray
la	recuperación	recovery
la	rubeola	German measles
la	silla de ruedas	wheelchair
la	tos	cough
la	tos ferina	whooping cough
la	transfusión (de sangre) (*pl* transfusiones (~~))	blood transfusion
la	varicela	chickenpox
la	viruela	smallpox

USEFUL PHRASES

curar to cure; curarse to get better
gravemente herido(a) seriously injured
¿tiene seguro? are you insured?
estoy resfriado(a) I have a cold
¡eso duele! that hurts!; me duele it hurts!
respirar to breathe
desmayarse to faint
toser to cough
morir to die
perder el conocimiento to lose consciousness
llevar el brazo en cabestrillo to have one's arm in a sling

ESSENTIAL WORDS *(masculine)*

el	**almuerzo**	lunch
el	**ascensor**	lift
el	**balcón** *(pl* balcones)	balcony
los	**baños públicos** *(LAm)*	toilets
el	**bar**	bar
el	**camarero**	waiter
el	**cambio**	change
el	**cheque**	cheque
el	**cuarto de baño**	bathroom
el	**depósito**	deposit
el	**desayuno**	breakfast
el	**director**	manager
el	**equipaje**	luggage
el	**hotel**	hotel
el	**huésped**	guest
el	**impreso**	form
el	**maletero**	porter
el	**número**	number
el	**pasaporte**	passport
el	**piso**	floor; storey
el	**precio**	price
el	**recepcionista**	receptionist
el	**restaurante**	restaurant
el	**ruido**	noise
los	**servicios**	toilets
el	**teléfono**	telephone

USEFUL PHRASES

quisiera reservar una habitación I would like to book a room
una habitación con ducha/con baño a room with a shower/
  with a bathroom
una habitación individual a single room
una habitación doble a double room

ESSENTIAL WORDS *(feminine)*

la	cama de matrimonio	double bed
la	camarera	waitress
las	camas separadas	twin beds
la	comida	lunch; meal
la	comodidad	comfort
la	cuenta	bill
la	directora	manager
la	ducha	shower
la	entrada	entrance
la	escalera	stairs
la	estancia	stay
la	fecha	date
la	ficha	form
la	habitación *(pl* habitaciones)	room
la	huésped	guest
la	llave	key
la	maleta	suitcase
la	media pensión	half board
la	noche	night
la	pensión *(pl* pensiones)	guest house
la	pensión completa	full board
la	piscina	swimming pool
la	planta	floor; storey
la	planta baja	ground floor
la	recepción	reception
la	recepcionista	receptionist
la	salida de incendios	fire escape
la	tarifa	rate, rates
la	televisión *(pl* televisiones)	television
la	vista	view

USEFUL PHRASES

¿lleva algún documento de identidad? do you have any ID?
¿a qué hora se sirve el desayuno? what time is breakfast served?
limpiar la habitación to clean the room
"se ruega no molestar" "do not disturb"

IMPORTANT WORDS *(masculine)*

el	**albergue**	inn
el	**baño**	bathroom
el	**interruptor**	switch
el	**lavabo**	washbasin; bathroom
el	**precio total**	inclusive price
el	**recibo**	receipt

USEFUL WORDS *(masculine)*

el	**cocinero**	cook
el	**maître**	head waiter
el	**sumiller**	wine waiter
el	**vestíbulo**	foyer

USEFUL PHRASES

ocupado(a) occupied
libre vacant
limpio(a) clean
sucio(a) dirty
dormir to sleep
despertar to wake
"con todas las comodidades" "with all facilities"
¿podrían despertarme (*or* llamarme) mañana por la mañana a las siete? I'd
    like a 7 o'clock alarm call tomorrow morning, please
una habitación con vistas al mar a room overlooking the sea

IMPORTANT WORDS *(feminine)*

la	**bañera**	bathtub
la	**bienvenida**	welcome
la	**camarera (de habitaciones)**	chambermaid
la	**casa de huéspedes**	guest house
la	**factura**	bill
la	**guía turística**	guidebook
la	**propina**	tip
la	**reclamación** (*pl* reclamaciones)	complaint

USEFUL WORDS *(feminine)*

la	**cocinera**	cook

USEFUL PHRASES

una habitación con media pensión **room with half board**
¿nos sentamos fuera *or* en la terraza? **shall we sit outside?**
nos sirvieron la cena fuera *or* en la terraza **we were served dinner outside**
un hotel de tres estrellas **a three-star hotel**
IVA incluido **inclusive of VAT**

ESSENTIAL WORDS *(masculine)*

el	**aparcamiento** *(Sp)*	car park; parking space
el	**apartamento**	flat, apartment
el	**ascensor**	lift
el	**balcón** *(pl balcones)*	balcony
el	**bloque de departamentos** *(LAm)*	block of flats
el	**bloque de pisos** *(Sp)*	block of flats
el	**comedor**	dining room
el	**cuarto de baño**	bathroom
el	**departamento** *(LAm)*	flat, apartment
el	**dormitorio**	bedroom
el	**edificio**	building
el	**estacionamiento** *(LAm)*	car park; parking space
el	**exterior**	exterior
el	**garaje**	garage
el	**interior**	interior
el	**jardín** *(pl jardines)*	garden
el	**mueble**	piece of furniture
los	**muebles**	furniture
el	**numéro de teléfono**	phone number
el	**patio**	yard
el	**piso**	floor, storey; *(Sp)* flat, apartment
el	**pueblo**	village
el	**salón** *(pl salones)*	living room
el	**sótano**	basement
el	**terreno**	plot of land

USEFUL PHRASES

cuando vaya a casa when I go home
mirar por la ventana to look out of the window
en mi/tu/nuestra casa at my/your/our house
mudarse de casa to move house
alquilar un apartamento *or* un piso to rent a flat

ESSENTIAL WORDS *(feminine)*

la	**avenida**	avenue
la	**bodega**	cellar
la	**calefacción (central)**	(central) heating
	(pl calefacciones (~es))	
la	**calle**	street
la	**casa**	house
la	**ciudad**	town; city
la	**cocina**	kitchen
la	**comodidad**	comfort
la	**dirección** *(pl* direcciones)	address
la	**ducha**	shower
la	**entrada**	entrance
la	**entrada para coches** *(Sp)*	drive
	or **para carros** *(LAm)*	
la	**escalera**	stairs
la	**habitación** *(pl* habitaciones)	room
la	**llave**	key
la	**parcela**	plot of land
la	**pared**	wall
la	**planta**	floor, storey
la	**planta baja**	ground floor
la	**plaza de parking** *or* **de garaje**	parking space *(in car park)*
la	**puerta**	door
la	**puerta principal**	front door
la	**sala de estar**	living room
la	**urbanización** *(pl* urbanizaciones)	housing estate
la	**ventana**	window
la	**vista**	view

USEFUL PHRASES

vivo en una casa/en un apartamento *or* un piso I live in a house /a flat
(en el piso de) arriba upstairs
(en el piso de) abajo downstairs
en el primer piso on the first floor
en la planta baja on the ground floor
en casa at home

IMPORTANT WORDS (*masculine*)

el	alojamiento	accommodation
el	alquiler	rent
el	baño	toilet
el	césped	lawn
el	dueño	landlord; owner
el	humo	smoke
el	lavabo	toilet; washbasin
el	mantenimiento	upkeep
el	mobiliario	furniture
el	pasillo	corridor
el	piso amueblado	furnished flat
el	portero	caretaker
el	propietario	owner; landlord
el	rellano	landing
el	tejado	roof
el	trastero	lumber room; (*Mex*) cupboard
el	vecino	neighbour

USEFUL WORDS (*masculine*)

el	ático	penthouse; attic
el	chalet (*pl* ~s)	bungalow; detached house
el	cristal	window pane
el	despacho	study
el	escalón (*pl* escalones)	step
el	estudio	studio flat
el	inquilino	tenant; lodger
el	muro	wall
el	parquet (*pl* ~s)	parquet floor
el	piso piloto	show flat
el	seto	hedge
el	suelo	floor
el	techo	ceiling
el	timbre	door bell
el	tragaluz (*pl* tragaluces)	skylight
el	umbral	doorstep
el	vestíbulo	hall
el	vidrio	window pane

IMPORTANT WORDS *(feminine)*

la	casa de campo	cottage
la	chimenea	chimney; fireplace
la	dueña	landlady; owner
la	mudanza	move
la	portera	caretaker
la	propietaria	owner; landlady
la	señora de la limpieza	cleaner
la	vecina	neighbour
la	vivienda	housing

USEFUL WORDS *(feminine)*

el	ama de casa *(f pl* amas ~~)	housewife
la	antena	aerial
la	baldosa	tile
la	buhardilla	attic
la	caldera	boiler
la	contraventana	shutter
la	cristalera *(Sp)*	French window
la	decoración *(pl* decoraciones)	decoration
la	fachada	front *(of house)*
la	habitación de los invitados	spare room
la	inquilina	tenant; lodger
la	persiana	blind
la	portería	caretaker's room
la	puerta ventana	French window
la	teja	roof tile; slate
la	tubería	pipe
la	vivienda de protección oficial	council flat *or* house

USEFUL PHRASES

llamar a la puerta to knock at the door
acaba de sonar el timbre the doorbell's just gone
desde fuera from the outside
dentro on the inside
hasta el techo up to the ceiling

ESSENTIAL WORDS *(masculine)*

el	**armario**	cupboard; wardrobe
el	**bote de la basura** (*Mex*)	dustbin
el	**buzón** (*pl* buzones)	letterbox
el	**cazo**	saucepan
el	**cenicero**	ashtray
el	**cepillo**	brush
el	**cuadro**	picture
el	**cubo de la basura**	dustbin
el	**despertador**	alarm clock
el	**espejo**	mirror
el	**fregadero**	sink
el	**frigorífico** (*Sp*)	fridge
el	**gas**	gas
el	**grifo**	tap
el	**interruptor**	switch
el	**jabón** (*pl* jabones)	soap
el	**lavabo**	washbasin; toilet
la	**pasta de dientes**	toothpaste
el	**póster** (*pl* ~es *or* ~s)	poster
el	**radiador**	radiator
el	**refrigerador** (*LAm*)	fridge
el	**televisor**	television set
el	**vídeo** (*Sp*) *or* video (*LAm*)	video recorder

USEFUL PHRASES

darse un baño, bañarse to have a bath
darse una ducha, ducharse to have a shower
hacer la limpieza de la casa to do the housework
me gusta cocinar I like cooking

ESSENTIAL WORDS *(feminine)*

el	agua *(f)*	water
la	alfombra	carpet, rug
la	almohada	pillow
la	balanza	scales
la	bandeja	tray
la	bañera	bath
la	cacerola	saucepan
la	cafetera	coffee pot; coffee maker
la	cazuela	saucepan
la	cocina	cooker
las	cortinas	curtains
la	ducha	shower
la	electricidad	electricity
la	foto	photo
la	lámpara	lamp
la	lavadora	washing machine
la	luz *(pl* luces*)*	light
la	manta	blanket
la	radio	radio
la	refrigeradora *(LAm)*	fridge
la	sábana	sheet
la	servilleta	napkin
las	tareas domésticas	housework
la	televisión *(pl* televisiones*)*	television
la	toalla	towel
la	vajilla	dishes

USEFUL PHRASES

ver la televisión to watch television
en televisión on television
encender/apagar la tele to switch on/off the TV
tirar algo al cubo de la basura to throw sth in the dustbin
lavar or fregar los platos to do the dishes

IMPORTANT WORDS (masculine)

el	**bidé**	bidet
el	**detergente (en polvo)**	washing powder
el	**enchufe**	plug; socket
el	**horno**	oven
el	**lavavajillas** (*pl inv*)	dishwasher; washing-up liquid
el	**mueble de cocina**	cooker
el	**polvo**	dust

USEFUL WORDS (masculine)

el	**adorno**	ornament
el	**almohadón** (*pl* almohadones)	bolster
el	**cojín** (*pl* cojines)	cushion
el	**cubo**	bucket
el	**edredón nórdico** (*pl* edredones ~s)	duvet
el	**horno microondas**	microwave oven
el	**jarrón** (*pl* jarrones)	vase
el	**molinillo de café**	coffee grinder
el	**paño de cocina**	dishcloth
el	**papel pintado**	wallpaper
el	**picaporte**	door handle
el	**trapo (del polvo)**	duster

USEFUL PHRASES

enchufar/desenchufar to plug in/to unplug
pasar la aspiradora to hoover
hacer la colada to do the washing

IMPORTANT WORDS *(feminine)*

la	aspiradora	vacuum cleaner
la	bombilla	light bulb
la	cerradura	lock
la	colada	(clean) washing
la	estufa	heater
la	pintura	paint; painting
la	receta	recipe
la	ropa de cama	bedclothes
la	ropa sucia	(dirty) washing, laundry
la	sartén *(pl* sartenes)	frying pan
la	señora de la limpieza	cleaner

USEFUL WORDS *(feminine)*

la	basura	rubbish
la	batidora	blender
la	bayeta	duster
la	escalera (de mano)	ladder
la	escoba	broom
la	esponja	sponge
la	manta eléctrica	electric blanket
la	moqueta	fitted carpet
la	olla a presión	pressure cooker
la	papelera	waste paper basket
la	percha	coat hanger
la	plancha	iron
la	tabla de planchar	ironing board
la	tapa	lid
la	tapicería	upholstery
la	tostadora	toaster

USEFUL PHRASES

barrer to sweep (up)

limpiar to clean

recoger uno sus cosas to tidy away one's things

dejar uno sus cosas por ahí tiradas to leave one's things lying about

ESSENTIAL WORDS *(masculine)*

el	**banco**	bank
el	**billete (de banco)**	banknote
el	**bolígrafo**	Biro®
el	**buzón** (*pl* buzones)	postbox
el	**cambio**	change
el	**carnet** *or* **carné de identidad** (*Sp*)	ID card
	(*pl* ~s ~ ~)	
el	**cartero**	postman
el	**céntimo de euro**	euro cent
el	**cheque**	cheque
el	**código postal**	postcode
el	**contrato telefónico**	phone contract
el	**correo electrónico**	email
el	**documento de identidad**	ID card
el	**empleado**	counter clerk
el	**error**	mistake
el	**euro**	euro
el	**fax**	fax; fax machine
el	**impreso**	form
el	**ingreso**	deposit
el	**justificante**	written proof
el	**mensaje de texto**	text message
el	**mostrador**	counter
el	**prefijo**	dialling code
el	**número**	number
el	**paquete**	parcel
el	**pasaporte**	passport
el	**precio**	price
el	**sello**	stamp
el	**sobre**	envelope
el	**teléfono**	telephone
el	**tono de marcado**	dialling tone

USEFUL PHRASES

el banco más cercano the nearest bank

quisiera cobrar un cheque/cambiar dinero I would like to cash a
  cheque/change some money

ESSENTIAL WORDS *(feminine)*

la	**caja**	check-out
la	**carta**	letter
la	**cartera**	postwoman; wallet; (*LAm*) handbag
la	**cédula de identidad** (*LAm*)	ID card
la	**compañía de teléfonos**	phone company
la	**dirección** (*pl* direcciones)	address
la	**empleada**	counter clerk
la	**firma**	signature
la	**información**	information; directory enquiries
la	**libra (esterlina)**	pound (sterling)
la	**llamada**	call
la	**oficina de correos**	post office
la	**oficina de información y turismo**	tourist information office
la	**pluma**	pen
la	**respuesta**	reply
la	**tarjeta de crédito**	credit card
la	**tarjeta de débito**	debit card
la	**(tarjeta) postal**	postcard

USEFUL PHRASES

una llamada telefónica a phone call

llamar a algn por teléfono, telefonear a algn to phone sb

descolgar el teléfono to lift the receiver

marcar (el número) to dial (the number)

hola – soy el Dr Pérez *or* el Dr Pérez al habla hello, this is Dr. Pérez

la línea está ocupada the line is engaged

no cuelgue hold the line

me he equivocado de número I got the wrong number

colgar to hang up

quisiera hacer una llamada internacional I'd like to make an international phone call

IMPORTANT WORDS *(masculine)*

el	**archivo adjunto**	attachment
el	**buzón de voz** (*pl* buzones ~~)	voicemail
el	**cheque de viaje**	traveller's cheque
el	**cibercafé**	internet café
el	**contestador (automático)**	answerphone
el	**correo**	mail
el	**crédito**	credit
el	**domicilio**	home address
el	**gasto**	expense
el	**impuesto**	tax
el	**mail** (*pl* ~s)	email
el	**monedero**	purse
el	**pago**	payment
el	**papel de carta**	writing paper
el	**recargo**	extra charge
el	**SMS** (*pl inv*)	text message
el	**talonario de cheques**	cheque book
el	**telefonista**	operator
el	**(teléfono) fijo**	landline
el	**(teléfono) móvil**	mobile (phone)
el	**telegrama**	telegram
el	**tipo de cambio**	exchange rate

USEFUL WORDS *(masculine)*

el	**apartado de correos**	PO box
el	**auricular**	receiver
el	**destinatario**	addressee
el	**documento adjunto**	attachment
el	**giro postal**	postal order
el	**nombre de acceso** (*or* **entrada**) **al sistema**	login
el	**papel de envolver**	wrapping paper
el	**remitente**	sender
el	**tono de llamada**	ringtone

IMPORTANT WORDS *(feminine)*

la	banda ancha	broadband
la	cabina telefónica	callbox
la	contraseña	password
la	cuenta (bancaria)	(bank) account
la	estampilla	stamp
la	guía telefónica	telephone directory
la	llamada telefónica	phone call
la	oficina de objetos perdidos	lost property office
la	peseta	peseta
la	ranura	slot
la	recogida	collection
la	recompensa	reward
la	tarjeta telefónica	(*prepaid*) phonecard
la	tarjeta de recarga (del móvil)	top-up (card)
la	telefonista	operator

USEFUL WORDS *(feminine)*

la	carta certificada	registered letter
la	destinataria	addressee
la	llamada internacional	international call
la	llamada local	local call
la	llamada nacional	inter-city call
la	oficina de cambio	bureau de change
la	remitente	sender
la	tarjeta SIM (*pl* ~s ~)	SIM card

USEFUL PHRASES

he perdido la cartera I've lost my wallet
rellenar un impreso to fill in a form
en mayúsculas in block letters
hacer una llamada a cobro revertido to make a reverse charge call

GENERAL SITUATIONS

¿cuál es su dirección? what is your address?
¿cómo se escribe? how do you spell that?
¿tiene cambio de 100 euros? do you have change of 100 euros?
escribir to write
responder to reply
firmar to sign
¿me puede ayudar por favor? can you help me please?
¿cómo se va a la estación? how do I get to the station?
todo recto straight on
a la derecha to *or* on the right; **a la izquierda** to *or* on the left

LETTERS

Querido Carlos Dear Carlos
Querida Ana Dear Ana
Estimado señor Dear Sir
Estimada señora Dear Madam
recuerdos, saludos best wishes
un abrazo de, un beso de, besos de love from
le saluda atentamente *or* **cordialmente** kind regards
besos y abrazos love and kisses
atentamente yours faithfully
reciba un atento saludo, le saluda atentamente yours sincerely
sigue PTO

E-MAILS

mandarle un correo electrónico a algn to mail *or* email sb

MOBILES

mandarle un mensaje de texto a algn to text sb

PRONUNCIATION GUIDE

Pronounced approximately as:

A	ah
B	bay
C	thay, say
D	day
E	ay
F	efay
G	khay
H	atchay
I	ee
J	khota
K	kah
L	elay
LL	elyay
M	emay
N	enay
Ñ	enyay
O	oh
P	pay
Q	koo
R	eray
S	essay
T	tay
U	oo
V	oobay (*Sp*), bay korta (*LAm*)
W	oobay doblay (*Sp*), doblay bay (*LAm*)
X	ekees
Y	ee griayga
Z	theta, seta

ESSENTIAL WORDS (masculine)

el	abogado	lawyer
el	accidente	accident
el	carnet de identidad (Sp) (pl ~s ~ ~)	ID card
el	documento de identidad	ID card
el	incendio	fire
el	policía	policeman
el	problema	problem
el	robo	burglary; theft

IMPORTANT WORDS (masculine)

el	atracador	armed robber; mugger
el	atraco	hold-up; mugging
el	consulado	consulate
el	control policial	checkpoint; roadblock
el	culpable	culprit
el	daño or los daños	damage
el	ejército	army
el	espía	spy
el	gobierno	government
el	guardia civil	civil guard (person)
los	impuestos	income tax
el	ladrón (pl ladrones)	burglar; thief; robber
el	monedero	purse
el	muerto	dead man
el	permiso	permission
el	propietario	owner
el	testigo	witness

USEFUL PHRASES

robar to burgle; to steal; to rob
¡me han robado la cartera! someone has stolen my wallet!
ilegal illegal; inocente innocent
no es culpa mía it's not my fault
¡socorro! help!; ¡al ladrón! stop thief!
¡fuego! fire!; ¡arriba las manos! hands up!
robar un banco to rob a bank
encarcelar to imprison; fugarse, escapar to escape

ESSENTIAL WORDS *(feminine)*

la	**abogada**	lawyer
la	**cédula de identidad** *(LAm)*	identity card
la	**culpa**	fault
la	**documentación**	papers
la	**identidad**	identity
la	**policía**	police; policewoman
la	**verdad**	truth

IMPORTANT WORDS *(feminine)*

la	**atracadora**	armed robber; mugger
la	**banda**	gang
la	**cartera**	wallet; *(LAm)* handbag
la	**comisaría**	police station
la	**culpable**	culprit
la	**denuncia**	report
la	**espía**	spy
la	**Guardia Civil**	Civil Guard
la	**guardia civil**	civil guard *(person)*
la	**ladrona**	burglar; thief; robber
la	**manifestación** *(pl* manifestaciones*)*	demonstration
la	**muerta**	dead woman
la	**muerte**	death
la	**multa**	fine
la	**pena de muerte**	death penalty
la	**póliza de seguros**	insurance policy
la	**propietaria**	owner
la	**recompensa**	reward
la	**testigo**	witness

USEFUL PHRASES

un atraco a mano armada a hold-up
raptar *or* secuestrar a un niño to abduct a child
un grupo de gamberros a bunch of hooligans
en la cárcel in prison
pelearse to fight; arrestar to arrest; acusar to charge
estar detenido(a) to be remanded in custody
acusar a algn de algo to accuse sb of sth; to charge sb with sth

USEFUL WORDS (*masculine*)

el	**arresto**	arrest
el	**asesinato**	murder
el	**asesino**	murderer
el	**botín** (*pl* botines)	loot
el	**cadáver**	corpse
el	**crimen** (*pl* crímenes)	murder; crime
el	**criminal**	criminal
el	**detective privado**	private detective
el	**disparo (de arma)**	(gun) shot
el	**drogadicto**	drug addict
el	**encarcelamiento**	imprisonment
el	**estafador**	crook
el	**gamberro**	hooligan
el	**gángster** (*pl* ~s)	gangster
el	**guarda**	guard; warden
el	**guardia**	guard; policeman
el	**inmigrante ilegal**	illegal immigrant
el	**intento**	attempt
el	**juez** (*pl* jueces)	judge
el	**juicio**	trial
el	**jurado**	jury
el	**levantamiento**	uprising
el	**pirómano**	arsonist
el	**poli**	cop
el	**preso**	prisoner
el	**rehén** (*pl* rehenes)	hostage
el	**rescate**	ransom; rescue
el	**revólver**	revolver
el	**secuestrador**	kidnapper; hijacker
el	**secuestro**	kidnapping
el	**secuestro aéreo**	hijacking
el	**terrorismo**	terrorism
el	**terrorista**	terrorist
el	**traficante de drogas**	drug dealer
el	**tribunal**	court
los	**tribunales**	law courts
el	**valor**	bravery

USEFUL WORDS (feminine)

la	**acusación** (pl acusaciones)	the prosecution; charge
el	**arma** (pl f las **armas**)	weapon
la	**asesina**	murderer
la	**bomba**	bomb
la	**cárcel**	prison
la	**celda**	cell
la	**criminal**	criminal
la	**declaración** (pl declaraciones)	statement
la	**defensa**	defence
la	**detective privada**	private detective
la	**detención** (pl detenciones)	arrest
la	**droga**	drug
la	**drogadicta**	drug addict
la	**estafadora**	crook
la	**fuga**	escape
la	**gamberra**	hooligan
la	**guarda**	guard; warden
la	**guardia**	guard; policewoman
la	**inmigrante ilegal**	illegal immigrant
la	**investigación** (pl investigaciones)	inquiry
la	**ley**	law
la	**multa**	fine
la	**pelea**	fight
la	**pirómana**	arsonist
la	**pistola**	gun
la	**poli**	the cops; cop
la	**prisión** (pl prisiones)	prison
la	**presa**	prisoner
la	**prueba**	proof
las	**pruebas**	evidence
la	**redada**	raid
la	**rehén** (pl rehenes)	hostage
la	**riña**	argument
la	**secuestradora**	kidnapper; hijacker
la	**suplantación de personalidad** (pl suplantaciones ~ ~)	identity theft
la	**terrorista**	terrorist
la	**traficante de drogas**	drug dealer

ESSENTIAL WORDS *(masculine)*

el **acero**	steel
el **algodón**	cotton
el **caucho**	rubber
el **cristal**	glass
el **cuero**	leather
el **gas**	gas
el **gasoil**	diesel
el **hierro**	iron
el **metal**	metal
el **oro**	gold
el **plástico**	plastic
el **vidrio**	glass

IMPORTANT WORDS *(masculine)*

el **acero inoxidable**	stainless steel
el **aluminio**	aluminium
el **cartón**	cardboard
el **estado**	condition
el **hierro forjado**	wrought iron
el **ladrillo**	brick
el **papel**	paper
el **tejido**	fabric

USEFUL PHRASES

una silla de madera a wooden chair
una caja de plástico a plastic box
un anillo de oro a gold ring
en buen estado, en buenas condiciones in good condition
en mal estado, en malas condiciones in bad condition

ESSENTIAL WORDS *(feminine)*

la	**lana**	wool
la	**madera**	wood
la	**piedra**	stone
la	**piel**	fur; leather
la	**plata**	silver
la	**tela**	fabric

IMPORTANT WORDS *(feminine)*

la	**fibra sintética**	synthetic fibre
la	**seda**	silk

USEFUL PHRASES

un abrigo de piel **a fur coat**
un jersey de lana **a woollen jumper**
oxidado(a) **rusty**

USEFUL WORDS *(masculine)*

el acrílico	acrylic
el alambre	wire
el ante	suede
el bronce	bronze
el carbón	coal
el cemento	concrete
el cobre	copper
el encaje	lace
el estaño	tin
el hilo	thread
el latón	brass
el lino	linen
el líquido	liquid
el mármol	marble
el material	material
el mimbre	wickerwork
el pegamento	glue
el plomo	lead
el raso	satin
el terciopelo	velvet
el tweed	tweed

USEFUL WORDS (*feminine*)

la	**arcilla**	clay
la	**cera**	wax
la	**cerámica**	ceramics
la	**cola**	glue
la	**cuerda**	string
la	**escayola**	plaster
la	**gomaespuma**	foam rubber
la	**hojalata**	tin, tinplate
la	**lona**	canvas
la	**loza**	pottery
la	**paja**	straw
la	**pana**	corduroy
la	**porcelana**	china

ESSENTIAL WORDS (*masculine*)

el	director de orquesta	conductor
el	grupo	band
el	instrumento musical	musical instrument
el	músico	musician
el	piano	piano
el	violín (*pl* violines)	violin

USEFUL WORDS (*masculine*)

el	acorde	chord
el	acordeón (*pl* acordeones)	accordion
el	arco	bow
el	atril	music stand
el	bombo	bass drum
el	clarinete	clarinet
el	contrabajo	double bass
el	estuche	case
el	estudio de grabación	recording studio
el	fagot	bassoon
los	instrumentos de cuerda	string instruments
los	instrumentos de percusión	percussion instruments
los	instrumentos de viento	wind instruments
el	jazz	jazz
los	metales	brass
el	micrófono	microphone
el	minidisco	minidisc
el	oboe	oboe
el	órgano	organ
los	platillos	cymbals
el	saxofón (*pl* saxofones)	saxophone
el	solfeo	music theory
el	solista	soloist
el	tambor	drum
el	triángulo	triangle
el	trombón (*pl* trombones)	trombone
el	violonchelo	cello

ESSENTIAL WORDS (feminine)

la	batería	drums, drum kit
la	directora de orquesta	conductor
la	flauta	flute
la	flauta dulce	recorder
la	guitarra	guitar
la	música	music; musician
la	orquesta	orchestra

USEFUL WORDS (feminine)

la	armónica	harmonica
el	arpa	harpe
la	batuta	conductor's baton
la	composición (pl composiciones)	composition
la	corneta	bugle
la	cuerda	string
la	gaita	bagpipes
la	grabación digital (pl grabaciones ~es)	digital recording
la	megafonía	PA system
la	mesa de mezclas	mixing deck
la	nota	note
la	pandereta	tambourine
la	solista	soloist
la	tecla (de piano)	(piano) key
la	trompeta	trumpet
la	viola	viola

USEFUL PHRASES

tocar or interpretar una pieza to play a piece
tocar alto/bajo to play loudly/softly
tocar afinado/desafinado to play in tune/out of tune
tocar el piano/la guitarra to play the piano/the guitar
tocar la batería to play drums
Pedro a la batería Pedro on drums
practicar el piano to practise the piano
¿tocas en un grupo? do you play in a band?
una nota falsa a wrong note

CARDINAL NUMBERS

cero	0	zero
uno (m), una (f)	1	one
dos	2	two
tres	3	three
cuatro	4	four
cinco	5	five
seis	6	six
siete	7	seven
ocho	8	eight
nueve	9	nine
diez	10	ten
once	11	eleven
doce	12	twelve
trece	13	thirteen
catorce	14	fourteen
quince	15	fifteen
dieciséis	16	sixteen
diecisiete	17	seventeen
dieciocho	18	eighteen
diecinueve	19	nineteen
veinte	20	twenty
veintiuno(a)	21	twenty-one
veintidós	22	twenty-two
veintitrés	23	twenty-three
treinta	30	thirty
treinta y uno(a)	31	thirty-one
treinta y dos	32	thirty-two
cuarenta	40	forty
cincuenta	50	fifty
sesenta	60	sixty
setenta	70	seventy
ochenta	80	eighty
noventa	90	ninety
cien	100	one hundred

CARDINAL NUMBERS *(continued)*

ciento uno(a)	101	a hundred and one
ciento dos	102	a hundred and two
ciento diez	110	a hundred and ten
ciento ochenta y dos	182	a hundred and eighty-two
doscientos(as)	200	two hundred
doscientos(as) uno(a)	201	two hundred and one
doscientos(as) dos	202	two hundred and two
trescientos(as)	300	three hundred
cuatrocientos(as)	400	four hundred
quinientos(as)	500	five hundred
seiscientos(as)	600	six hundred
setecientos(as)	700	seven hundred
ochocientos(as)	800	eight hundred
novecientos(as)	900	nine hundred
mil	1000	one thousand
mil uno(a)	1001	a thousand and one
mil dos	1002	a thousand and two
dos mil	2000	two thousand
dos mil seis	2006	two thousand and six
diez mil	10000	ten thousand
cien mil	100000	one hundred thousand
un millón	1000000	one million
dos millones	2000000	two million

USEFUL PHRASES

mil euros a thousand euros
un millón de dólares one million dollars
tres coma dos (3,2) three point two (3.2)

ORDINAL NUMBERS

primero(a)	$1^{\underline{o}}, 1^{\underline{a}}$	first
segundo(a)	$2^{\underline{o}}, 2^{\underline{a}}$	second
tercero(a)	$3^{\underline{o}}, 3^{\underline{a}}$	third
cuarto(a)	$4^{\underline{o}}, 4^{\underline{a}}$	fourth
quinto(a)	$5^{\underline{o}}, 5^{\underline{a}}$	fifth
sexto(a)	$6^{\underline{o}}, 6^{\underline{a}}$	sixth
séptimo(a)	$7^{\underline{o}}, 7^{\underline{a}}$	seventh
octavo(a)	$8^{\underline{o}}, 8^{\underline{a}}$	eighth
noveno(a)	$9^{\underline{o}}, 9^{\underline{a}}$	ninth
décimo(a)	$10^{\underline{o}}, 10^{\underline{a}}$	tenth
undécimo(a)	$11^{\underline{o}}, 11^{\underline{a}}$	eleventh
duodécimo(a)	$12^{\underline{o}}, 12^{\underline{a}}$	twelfth
decimotercero(a)	$13^{\underline{o}}, 13^{\underline{a}}$	thirteenth
decimocuarto(a)	$14^{\underline{o}}, 14^{\underline{a}}$	fourteenth
decimoquinto(a)	$15^{\underline{o}}, 15^{\underline{a}}$	fifteenth
decimosexto(a)	$16^{\underline{o}}, 16^{\underline{a}}$	sixteenth
decimoséptimo(a)	$17^{\underline{o}}, 17^{\underline{a}}$	seventeenth
decimoctavo(a)	$18^{\underline{o}}, 18^{\underline{a}}$	eighteenth
decimonoveno(a), decimonono(a)	$19^{\underline{o}}, 19^{\underline{a}}$	nineteenth
vigésimo(a)	$20^{\underline{o}}, 20^{\underline{a}}$	twentieth

Note:
Ordinal numbers are hardly ever used above 10th in spoken Spanish, and rarely at all above 20th. It's normal to use the cardinal numbers instead, except for **milésimo(a)**.

milésimo(a)	$1000^{\underline{o}}, 1000^{\underline{a}}$	thousandth
dos milésimo(a)	$2000^{\underline{o}}, 2000^{\underline{a}}$	two thousandth
millonésimo(a)	$1000000^{\underline{o}}, 1000000^{\underline{a}}$	millionth
dos millonésimo(a)	$2000000^{\underline{o}}, 2000000^{\underline{a}}$	two millionth

FRACTIONS

un medio	$\frac{1}{2}$	a half
uno(a) y medio(a)	$1\frac{1}{2}$	one and a half
dos y medio(a)	$2\frac{1}{2}$	two and a half
un tercio, la tercera parte	$\frac{1}{3}$	a third
dos tercios, las dos terceras partes	$\frac{2}{3}$	two thirds
un cuarto, la cuarta parte	$\frac{1}{4}$	a quarter
tres cuartos, las tres cuartas partes	$\frac{3}{4}$	three quarters
un sexto, la sexta parte	$\frac{1}{6}$	a sixth
tres y cinco sextos	$3\frac{5}{6}$	three and five sixths
un séptimo, la séptima parte	$\frac{1}{7}$	a seventh
un octavo, la octava parte	$\frac{1}{8}$	an eighth
un noveno, la novena parte	$\frac{1}{9}$	a ninth
un décimo, la décima parte	$\frac{1}{10}$	a tenth
un onceavo, la onceava parte	$\frac{1}{11}$	an eleventh
un doceavo, la doceava parte	$\frac{1}{12}$	a twelfth
siete doceavos, las siete doceavas partes	$\frac{7}{12}$	seven twelfths
un centésimo, la centésima parte	$\frac{1}{100}$	a hundredth
un milésimo, la milésima parte	$\frac{1}{1000}$	a thousandth

USEFUL PHRASES

ambos (*f* ambas), los dos (*f* las dos) both of them
un bocado de a mouthful of
un bote de a jar of; a tin *or* can of
una botella de a bottle of
un botellín (de cerveza) a small bottle (of beer)
una caja de a box of
(gran) cantidad de lots of
una caña (de cerveza) a small glass of beer
cien gramos de a hundred grammes of
un centenar de (about) a hundred
un cuarto de a quarter of
tres cuartos de three quarters of
una cucharada de a spoonful of
una docena de (about) a dozen
un grupo de a group of
una jarra de a jug of; a mug of (*beer*)
un kilo de a kilo of
un litro de a litre of
la mayoría (de), la mayor parte (de) most (of)
media docena de half a dozen
medio litro de half a litre of
una loncha de jamón a slice of ham
un metro de a metre of
miles de thousands of

USEFUL PHRASES

la mitad de half of
un montón de a pile of
mucho(a) a lot of, much
muchos (f muchas) a lot of, many
multitud de, montones de loads of
un paquete de a packet of
un par de a pair of
un plato de a plate of
un poco de a little; some
una porción de a portion of
un puñado de a handful of
una rebanada de pan a slice of bread
un rebaño de a herd of (*cattle*); a flock of (*sheep*)
una rodaja de merluza a slice of hake
un sobre de sopa a packet of soup
una taza de a cup of
un tazón de a bowl of
un terrón de azúcar a lump of sugar
un tonel de a barrel of
un trozo de papel/pastel a piece of paper/cake
a unos metros de a few metres from
un vaso de a glass of
varios several
a varios kilómetros de a few kilometres from

ESSENTIAL WORDS *(masculine)*

el	anillo	ring
el	cepillo	brush
el	cepillo de dientes	toothbrush
el	champú	shampoo
el	desodorante	deodorant
el	espejo	mirror
el	maquillaje	make-up
el	peine	comb
el	perfume	perfume
el	reloj	watch

USEFUL WORDS *(masculine)*

el	aftershave	aftershave
el	broche	brooch
el	colgante	pendant
el	collar	necklace
el	dentífrico	toothpaste
el	diamante	diamond
los	efectos personales	personal effects
el	esmalte (de uñas)	nail varnish
el	gemelo	cufflink
el	kleenex® (pl inv)	tissue
el	lápiz de labios (pl lápices ~ ~)	lipstick
el	llavero	key-ring
el	maquillaje	make-up
el	neceser	toilet bag
el	papel higiénico	toilet paper
el	peinado	hairstyle
el	pendiente	earring
los	polvos compactos	face powder
los	polvos para la cara	face powder
el	quitaesmalte	nail varnish remover
el	rímel	mascara
el	rulo	roller
el	secador	hairdryer

ESSENTIAL WORDS (feminine)

el	agua de colonia (f)	eau de toilette
la	cadena	chain
la	crema para la cara	face cream
la	cuchilla de afeitar	razor
la	joya	jewel
la	maquinilla de afeitar	(safety) razor
la	pasta de dientes	toothpaste
la	pulsera	bracelet

USEFUL WORDS (feminine)

la	alianza	wedding ring
la	base de maquillaje	foundation
la	brocha de afeitar	shaving brush
la	crema de afeitar	shaving cream
la	esponja	sponge
la	espuma de afeitar	shaving foam
la	manicura	manicure
la	perla	pearl
la	polvera	(powder) compact
la	sombra de ojos	eye shadow

USEFUL PHRASES

maquillarse to put on one's make-up
desmaquillarse to take off one's make-up
hacerse un peinado to do one's hair
peinarse to comb one's hair
cepillarse el pelo to brush one's hair
afeitarse to shave
lavarse los dientes, limpiarse los dientes to clean or brush one's teeth

ESSENTIAL WORDS (*masculine*)

el	**árbol**	tree
el	**césped**	lawn
el	**jardín** (*pl* jardines)	garden
el	**jardinero**	gardener
el	**sol**	sun

IMPORTANT WORDS (*masculine*)

el	**arbusto**	bush
el	**banco**	bench
el	**camino**	path
el	**cultivo**	cultivation; crop
el	**ramo de flores**	bunch of flowers

USEFUL PHRASES

plantar to plant
quitar las malas hierbas, desherbar to weed
regalar a algn un ramo de flores to give sb a bunch of flowers
cortar el césped to mow the lawn
"no pisar el césped" "keep off the grass"
a mi padre le gusta la jardinería my father likes gardening

ESSENTIAL WORDS *(feminine)*

la	**flor**	flower
la	**hierba**	grass
la	**hoja**	leaf
la	**jardinera**	gardener; flower bed
la	**jardinería**	gardening
la	**lluvia**	rain
la	**planta**	plant
la	**rama**	branch
la	**rosa**	rose
la	**tierra**	land; soil; ground
las	**verduras**	vegetables

IMPORTANT WORDS *(feminine)*

la	**abeja**	bee
la	**avispa**	wasp
las	**malas hierbas**	weeds
la	**raíz** (*pl* raíces)	root
la	**sombra**	shade; shadow
la	**valla**	fence
la	**verja**	gate

USEFUL PHRASES

las flores están creciendo the flowers are growing
en el suelo on the ground
regar las plantas to water the flowers
coger flores to pick flowers
irse a la sombra to go into the shade
quedarse en la sombra to remain in the shade
a la sombra de un árbol in the shade of a tree

USEFUL WORDS (*masculine*)

el	**arriate**	flowerbed
el	**azafrán** (*pl* azafranes)	crocus
el	**brote**	bud
el	**clavel**	carnation
el	**cortacésped**	lawnmower
el	**crisantemo**	chrysanthemum
el	**diente de león**	dandelion
el	**estanque**	(ornamental) pool
el	**follaje**	leaves
el	**girasol**	sunflower
el	**gusano**	worm
el	**huerto**	vegetable garden
el	**invernadero**	greenhouse
el	**invierno**	winter
el	**jacinto**	hyacinth
el	**lirio**	lily
el	**lirio del valle**	lily of the valley
el	**narciso**	daffodil
el	**otoño**	autumn, fall
el	**parterre**	flowerbed
el	**pensamiento**	pansy
el	**ranúnculo**	buttercup
el	**rocío**	dew
el	**rosal**	rose bush
el	**sendero**	path
el	**seto**	hedge
el	**suelo**	ground; soil
el	**tallo**	stalk
el	**tronco**	trunk (*of tree*)
el	**tulipán** (*pl* tulipanes)	tulip
el	**verano**	summer

USEFUL WORDS *(feminine)*

la	amapola	poppy
la	baya	berry
la	campanilla	campanula, bellflower
la	campanilla de invierno	snowdrop
la	carretilla	wheelbarrow
la	cerca	fence
la	cosecha	crop
la	espina	thorn
la	herramienta	tool
la	hiedra	ivy
la	hortensia	hydrangea
las	lilas	lilac
la	madreselva	honeysuckle
la	manguera	hose
la	margarita	daisy
la	mariposa	butterfly
la	orquídea	orchid
la	peonía	peony
la	primavera	spring; primrose
la	regadera	watering can
la	semilla	seed
la	violeta	violet

ESSENTIAL WORDS (masculine)

los	anteojos de sol (LAm)	sunglasses
el	bañador	swimming trunks; swimsuit
el	bañista	swimmer
el	barco	boat; ship
el	barco de pesca	fishing boat
el	bikini	bikini
el	bote	boat
el	mar	sea
el	muelle	quay
el	paseo	walk
el	pescador	fisherman
el	pesquero	fishing boat
el	picnic (pl ~s)	picnic
el	puerto	port, harbour
el	puerto deportivo	marina
el	remo	rowing; oar
el	traje de baño	swimming trunks; swimsuit

IMPORTANT WORDS (masculine)

el	cangrejo	crab
el	castillo de arena	sandcastle
el	fondo	bottom
el	horizonte	horizon
el	mareo	seasickness
el	veraneante	holiday-maker

USEFUL PHRASES

en la playa at the seaside; at or on the beach
en el horizonte on the horizon
está mareado he is seasick
nadar to swim
ahogarse to drown
me voy a dar un baño I'm going for a swim
tirarse al agua, zambullirse to dive into the water
flotar to float

ESSENTIAL WORDS *(feminine)*

el	**agua** (*f*)	water
la	**arena**	sand
la	**bañista**	swimmer
la	**barca**	boat
la	**costa**	coast
las	**gafas de sol** (*Sp*)	sunglasses
la	**isla**	island
la	**natación**	swimming
la	**pescadora**	fisherwoman
la	**piedra**	stone
la	**playa**	beach; seaside
las	**quemaduras de sol**	sunburn
la	**toalla**	towel

IMPORTANT WORDS *(feminine)*

la	**colchoneta inflable**	airbed, lilo
la	**crema (de protección) solar**	suncream
la	**tabla de windsurf**	windsurfing board
la	**travesía**	crossing
la	**tumbona**	deckchair
la	**veraneante**	holiday-maker

USEFUL PHRASES

en el fondo del mar at the bottom of the sea
hacer la travesía en barco to go across by boat
broncearse, ponerse moreno(a) to get a tan
estar moreno(a) to be tanned
sabe nadar he can swim

USEFUL WORDS *(masculine)*

el	acantilado	cliff
el	aire de mar	sea air
el	balde	bucket
el	(barco de) vapor	steamer
los	binoculares	binoculars
el	bote de pedales	pedalo
el	cabo	headland
el	crucero	cruise
el	cubo	bucket
el	embarcadero	pier
el	estuario	estuary
el	faro	lighthouse
el	guijarro	pebble
el	marinero	sailor
el	marino	sailor; naval officer
el	mástil	mast
el	naufragio	shipwreck
los	náufragos	shipwrecked people, castaways
el	océano	ocean
el	oleaje	swell
el	pedal *(Sp)*	pedalo
los	prismáticos	binoculars
el	puente (de mando)	bridge *(of ship)*
los	restos de un naufragio	wreckage
el	salvavidas *(pl inv)*	lifeguard; lifebelt
el	socorrista	lifeguard
el	timón *(pl* timones)	rudder
el	transbordador	ferry

USEFUL WORDS *(feminine)*

las	**algas**	seaweed
el	**ancla** (*pl f* las **anclas**)	anchor
la	**bahía**	bay
la	**balsa**	raft
la	**bandera**	flag
la	**barca**	small boat
la	**boya**	buoy
la	**brisa marina**	sea breeze
la	**carga**	cargo
la	**concha**	shell
la	**corriente**	current
la	**desembocadura**	mouth (*of river*)
la	**espuma**	foam
la	**gaviota**	seagull
la	**insolación** (*pl* insolaciones)	sunstroke
la	**marea**	tide
la	**marina**	navy
la	**marinera**	sailor
la	**marina**	sailor; naval officer
la	**nave**	vessel
la	**ola**	wave
la	**orilla**	shore
la	**pala**	spade
la	**pasarela**	gangway
la	**ría**	estuary
la	**roca**	rock
la	**salvavidas** (*pl inv*) *or* **socorrista**	lifeguard
la	**sombrilla**	parasol
la	**tripulación** (*pl* tripulaciones)	crew
la	**vela**	sail; sailing

USEFUL PHRASES

tuve una insolación **I had sunstroke**
con la marea baja/alta **at low/high tide**
hacer vela **to go sailing**

ESSENTIAL WORDS *(masculine)*

el	**banco**	bank
el	**billete (de banco)**	banknote
el	**cambio**	change
el	**céntimo**	cent
el	**centro comercial**	shopping centre
el	**cheque**	cheque
el	**cliente**	customer
el	**departamento**	department
el	**dependiente**	shop assistant, sales assistant
el	**descuento**	discount
el	**dinero**	money
el	**estanco**	tobacconist's
el	**euro**	euro
los	**grandes almacenes**	department store
el	**hipermercado**	hypermarket
el	**mercado**	market
el	**número (de zapato)**	(shoe) size
el	**precio**	price
el	**regalo**	present
el	**souvenir** *(pl ~s)*	souvenir
el	**supermercado**	supermarket
el	**talonario de cheques**	cheque book
el	**vendedor**	salesman

USEFUL PHRASES

comprar/vender to buy/sell
¿cuánto cuesta? how much does it cost?
¿cuánto es? how much does it come to?
pagué veinte euros por esto, esto me costó veinte euros I paid 20 euros
   for that
en la carnicería/la panadería at the butcher's/bakery

ESSENTIAL WORDS *(feminine)*

la	agencia de viajes	travel agent's
la	alimentación	food
la	caja	checkout; cash desk
la	carnicería	butcher's
la	charcutería	pork butcher's
la	clienta	customer
la	compra	purchase
la	dependienta	shop assistant, sales assistant
la	farmacia	chemist's
la	floristería	flower shop
la	frutería	fruiterer's
la	lista	list
la	oficina de correos	post office
la	panadería	bakery
la	pastelería	cake shop
la	perfumería	perfume shop/department
la	pescadería	fishmonger's
la	rebaja	reduction
las	rebajas	sales
la	sección *(pl* secciones)	department
la	talla	size
la	tarjeta de crédito	credit card
la	tarjeta de débito	debit card
la	tienda	shop
la	tienda de alimentación *or* de comestibles	grocer's
la	vendedora	saleswoman
la	verdulería	greengrocer's
la	zapatería	shoe shop

IMPORTANT WORDS *(masculine)*

el	**artículo**	article
el	**carnicero**	butcher
el	**charcutero**	pork butcher
el	**comerciante**	shopkeeper
el	**comercio**	trade; shop
el	**comercio justo**	fair trade
el	**encargado**	manager
el	**frutero**	fruiterer
el	**mercadillo**	street market
el	**monedero**	purse
el	**mostrador**	counter
el	**panadero**	baker
el	**pastelero**	confectioner
el	**peluquero**	hairdresser
el	**pescadero**	fishmonger
el	**rastro** (*Sp*)	flea market
el	**recibo**	receipt
el	**tícket** (*pl* ~s)	receipt; ticket
el	**vendedor de periódicos**	newsagent
el	**verdulero**	greengrocer
el	**zapatero** .	cobbler

USEFUL PHRASES

sólo estoy mirando I'm just looking
es demasiado caro it's too expensive
algo más barato something cheaper
es barato it's cheap
"pague en caja" "pay at the checkout"
¿lo quiere para regalo? would you like it gift-wrapped?
debe de haber un error there must be some mistake

IMPORTANT WORDS *(feminine)*

la **biblioteca**	library
la **boutique**	boutique
la **calculadora**	calculator
la **carnicera**	butcher
la **cartera**	wallet; purse; (*LAm*) handbag
la **charcutera**	pork butcher
la **comerciante**	shopkeeper
la **encargada**	manager
la **escalera mecánica**	escalator
la **frutera**	fruiterer
la **librería**	bookshop
la **marca**	brand
la **panadera**	baker
la **pastelera**	confectioner
la **peluquera**	hairdresser
la **pescadera**	fishmonger
la **promoción** (*pl* promociones)	special offer
la **reclamación** (*pl* reclamaciones)	complaint
la **tintorería**	dry-cleaner's
la **vendedora de periódicos**	newsagent
la **verdulera**	greengrocer
la **vitrina**	display case; (*LAm*) shop window

USEFUL PHRASES

¿algo más? anything else?

S.A. (= *Sociedad Anónima*) Ltd

S.L. (= *Sociedad Limitada*) limited liability company

y Cía & Co

"de venta aquí" "on sale here"

un coche de ocasión a used car

en oferta, de oferta on special offer

el café de comercio justo fair-trade coffee

USEFUL WORDS *(masculine)*

el	**agente inmobiliario**	estate agent
el	**color**	colour
el	**escaparate**	shop window
el	**ferretero**	ironmonger
el	**gerente**	manager
el	**joyero**	jeweller; jewellery box
el	**librero**	bookseller
el	**óptico**	optician
el	**producto**	product
los	**productos**	produce
el	**recado**	errand
el	**relojero**	watchmaker; clockmaker
el	**tendero**	grocer
el	**trato**	deal
el	**videoclub** (*pl* ~s)	video shop

USEFUL PHRASES

ir a ver escaparates, ir de escaparates **to go window shopping**
horario **opening hours**
pagar en metálico **to pay cash**
pagar con un cheque **to pay by cheque**
pagar con tarjeta de crédito **to pay by credit card**

USEFUL WORDS *(feminine)*

la	**agencia de viajes**	travel agent's
la	**agencia inmobiliaria**	estate agent's
la	**agente inmobiliario**	estate agent
la	**caja de ahorros**	savings bank
la	**cola**	queue
la	**compra**	purchase; shopping
las	**compras**	shopping
la	**confitería**	sweetshop
la	**droguería**	hardware shop
la	**ferretera**	ironmonger
la	**ferretería**	ironmonger's
la	**gerente**	manager
la	**joyera**	jeweller
la	**joyería**	jeweller's
la	**lavandería**	laundry
la	**librera**	bookseller
la	**mercancía**	goods
la	**óptica**	optician; optician's
la	**papelería**	stationer's
la	**rebaja**	discount
la	**relojera**	watchmaker; clockmaker
la	**relojería**	watchmaker's; clockmaker's
la	**sucursal**	branch
la	**talla de cuello**	collar size
la	**tendera**	grocer
la	**venta**	sale

USEFUL PHRASES

en el escaparate in the window
ir de compras to go shopping
hacer la compra to do the shopping
gastar to spend

ESSENTIAL WORDS *(masculine)*

el	**aerobic**	aerobics
el	**ajedrez**	chess
el	**arco** *(LAm)*	goal
el	**balón** *(pl* balones)	ball *(large)*
el	**baloncesto**	basketball
el	**balonvolea**	volleyball
el	**billar**	billiards
el	**campeón** *(pl* campeones)	champion
el	**campeonato**	championship
el	**campo**	field, *(football)* pitch; *(golf)* course; *(basketball)* court
el	**ciclismo**	cycling
el	**críquet**	cricket
el	**deporte**	sport
el	**equipo**	team
el	**esquí**	skiing; ski
el	**esquí acuático**	water skiing
el	**estadio**	stadium
el	**fútbol**	football
el	**gimnasta**	gymnast
el	**golf**	golf
el	**hockey**	hockey
el	**juego**	game; play
el	**jugador**	player
el	**partido**	match, game
el	**paseo**	walk
el	**resultado**	result
el	**rugby**	rugby
el	**tenis**	tennis

USEFUL PHRASES

jugar al fútbol/tenis to play football/tennis
marcar un gol/un punto to score a goal/a point
llevar la cuenta de los tantos to keep the score
el campeón/la campeona del mundo the world champion
ganar/perder un partido to win/lose a match
mi deporte preferido my favourite sport

ESSENTIAL WORDS *(feminine)*

la	**campeona**	champion
la	**cancha**	(*basketball/tennis*) court; (*LAm*) field, (*football*) pitch
la	**cancha de tenis** (*LAm*)	tennis court
la	**equitación**	horse-riding
la	**gimnasia**	gymnastics
la	**gimnasta**	gymnast
la	**jugadora**	player
la	**natación**	swimming
la	**partida**	game (*chess etc*)
la	**pelota**	ball
la	**pesca**	fishing
la	**piscina**	swimming pool
la	**pista**	track
la	**pista de tenis** (*Sp*)	tennis court
la	**portería**	goal
la	**tabla de windsurf**	windsurfing board
la	**vela**	sailing; sail

USEFUL PHRASES

empatar to equalize; to draw
correr to run; saltar to jump; lanzar to throw
ganar *or* derrotar *or* vencer a algn to beat sb
entrenarse to train
el Liverpool gana por 2 a 1 Liverpool is leading by 2 goals to 1
un partido de tenis a game of tennis
es socio de un club he belongs to a club
ir de pesca to go fishing
ir a la piscina to go to the swimming pool
¿sabes nadar? can you swim?
hacer deporte to do sport
montar en bicicleta *or* hacer ciclismo to go cycling
hacer vela to go sailing
hacer footing/alpinismo to go jogging/climbing
patín de cuchilla/de ruedas/en línea (ice) skate/roller skate/Rollerblade®
tiro al arco/al blanco archery/target practice

IMPORTANT WORDS (*masculine*)

los	**bolos**	skittles
el	**encuentro**	match

USEFUL WORDS (*masculine*)

el	**adversario**	opponent
el	**alpinismo**	mountaineering
el	**árbitro**	referee; umpire (*tennis*)
el	**atletismo**	athletics
el	**bádminton**	badminton
el	**boxeo**	boxing
el	**buceo**	diving
el	**chándal**	tracksuit
el	**cronómetro**	stopwatch
el	**descanso**	half-time
el	**entrenador**	trainer; coach
el	**espectador**	spectator
el	**footing**	jogging
el	**ganador**	winner
el	**gol**	goal
el	**hipódromo**	race course
los	**Juegos Olímpicos**	Olympic Games
el	**Mundial (de Fútbol)**	World Cup
el	**parapente**	paragliding
el	**patín**	skate
el	**patinaje sobre hielo**	(ice) skating
el	**perdedor**	loser
el	**portero**	goalkeeper
el	**principiante**	beginner
el	**remo**	rowing; oar
el	**resultado**	score
el	**salto de altura**	high jump
el	**salto de longitud**	long jump
el	**squash**	squash
el	**tanto**	goal; point
el	**tiro**	shooting
el	**torneo**	tournament
el	**trineo**	sledge

IMPORTANT WORDS *(feminine)*

la	**bola**	ball (*small*)
la	**carrera**	race
las	**carreras (de caballos)**	horse-racing
la	**defensa**	defence
la	**petanca**	pétanque
la	**pista de esquí**	ski slope

USEFUL WORDS *(feminine)*

la	**adversaria**	opponent
la	**árbitra**	referee; umpire (*tennis*)
la	**camiseta (de deporte)**	jersey, shirt
la	**caña de pescar**	fishing rod
la	**caza**	hunting
la	**copa**	cup
la	**Copa del Mundo**	World Cup
la	**eliminatoria**	heat
la	**entrenadora**	trainer, coach
la	**esgrima**	fencing
la	**espectadora**	spectator
la	**estación de esquí**	ski resort
	(*pl* estaciones de ~)	
la	**etapa**	stage
la	**final**	final
la	**ganadora**	winner
la	**jabalina**	javelin
la	**lucha libre**	wrestling
la	**perdedora**	loser
la	**pesca**	fishing
la	**pista de hielo**	ice rink
la	**pista de patinaje**	skating rink
la	**portera**	goalkeeper
la	**principiante**	beginner
la	**prórroga**	extra time
la	**raqueta**	racket
la	**red**	net
la	**tribuna**	stand
las	**zapatillas de deporte**	sports shoes; trainers
las	**zapatillas de tenis**	tennis shoes

ESSENTIAL WORDS *(masculine)*

el	**actor**	actor
el	**ambiente**	atmosphere
el	**anfiteatro**	dress circle
el	**asiento**	seat
el	**auditorio**	auditorium; audience
el	**boleto** *(LAm)*	ticket
el	**cine**	cinema
el	**circo**	circus
el	**cómico**	comedian
el	**espectáculo**	show
el	**patio de butacas**	stalls
el	**payaso**	clown
el	**programa**	programme
el	**público**	audience
el	**teatro**	theatre
el	**vestuario**	costume
el	**videoclip** *(pl ~s)*	music video
el	**western** *(pl ~s)*	western

IMPORTANT WORDS *(masculine)*

el	**acomodador**	usher
el	**actor principal**	leading man
el	**ballet** *(pl ~s)*	ballet
el	**cartel**	notice; poster
el	**director**	director
el	**entreacto**	interval
el	**intermedio**	interval
el	**maquillaje**	make-up

USEFUL PHRASES

ir al teatro/al cine to go to the theatre/to the cinema
reservar un asiento to book a seat
un asiento en el patio de butacas a seat in the stalls
mi actor preferido/actriz preferida my favourite actor/actress
durante el intermedio during the interval
salir a escena to come on stage
interpretar el papel de to play the part of

ESSENTIAL WORDS (feminine)

la	**actriz** (pl actrices)	actress
la	**banda sonora**	soundtrack
la	**boletería** (LAm)	box office
la	**cómica**	comedian
la	**cortina**	curtain
la	**entrada**	ticket
la	**estrella de cine**	film star
la	**música**	music
la	**obra (de teatro)**	play
la	**ópera**	opera
la	**orquesta**	orchestra
la	**payasa**	clown
la	**película**	film
la	**sala**	auditorium; cinema
la	**salida**	exit
la	**sesión** (pl sesiones)	performance; showing
la	**taquilla**	box office

USEFUL PHRASES

interpretar to play
bailar to dance
cantar to sing
filmar una película to shoot a film
"próxima sesión: 21 horas" "next showing: 9 p.m."
"versión original" "original version"
"subtitulada" "subtitled"
"localidades agotadas" "full house"
aplaudir to clap
¡bis! encore!
¡bravo! bravo!
una película de ciencia ficción/de amor a science fiction film/a romance
una película de aventuras/de terror an adventure/horror film

IMPORTANT WORDS (*masculine continued*)

el	**primer actor**	leading man
el	**protagonista**	star
el	**subtítulo**	subtitle
el	**título**	title

USEFUL WORDS (*masculine*)

el	**anfiteatro**	circle
los	**aplausos**	applause
el	**apuntador**	prompter
el	**argumento**	plot
los	**bastidores**	wings
el	**crítico**	critic
el	**culebrón** (*pl* culebrones)	soap (opera)
el	**decorado**	scenery
el	**director de escena**	producer; stage manager
el	**dramaturgo**	playwright
el	**ensayo (general)**	(dress) rehearsal
el	**escenario**	stage; scene
el	**espectador**	member of the audience
el	**estrado**	platform
el	**estreno**	first night, premiere
el	**foco**	spotlight
el	**foso de la orquesta**	orchestra pit
el	**gallinero**	the "gods"
el	**guardarropa**	cloakroom
el	**guión** (*pl* guiones)	script
el	**guionista**	scriptwriter
el	**musical**	musical
el	**palco**	box
el	**papel**	part
el	**personaje**	character
el	**productor**	producer
el	**realizador**	director (*cinema*); producer (*TV*)
el	**regidor**	stage manager
el	**reparto**	cast
el	**serial**	serial
el	**vestíbulo**	foyer

IMPORTANT WORDS *(feminine)*

la	**acomodadora**	usherette
la	**actriz principal** *(pl* actrices ~es)	leading lady
la	**butaca**	seat
la	**cartelera**	hoarding, billboard; listings section
la	**comedia**	comedy
la	**directora**	director
la	**platea**	stalls
la	**primera actriz** *(pl* ~s actrices)	leading lady
la	**propina**	tip
la	**protagonista**	star
la	**reserva**	booking

USEFUL WORDS *(feminine)*

la	**actuación** *(pl* actuaciones)	acting, performance
la	**apuntadora**	prompter
las	**candilejas**	footlights
la	**crítica**	review; critics; critic
la	**directora de escena**	producer; stage manager
la	**dramaturga**	playwright
la	**escena**	scene
la	**escenografía**	scenery
la	**espectadora**	member of the audience
la	**farsa**	farce
la	**función** *(pl* funciones)	performance
la	**guionista**	scriptwriter
la	**pantalla**	screen
la	**platea**	stalls
la	**productora**	producer
la	**puesta en escena**	production
la	**realizadora**	director *(cinema)*; producer *(TV)*
la	**regidora**	stage manager
la	**representación** *(pl* representaciones)	performance
la	**serie**	series
la	**tragedia**	tragedy

ESSENTIAL WORDS *(masculine)*

el	**año**	year
el	**cuarto de hora**	quarter of an hour
el	**despertador**	alarm clock
el	**día**	day
el	**fin de semana**	weekend
el	**instante**	moment
el	**mes**	month
el	**minuto**	minute
el	**momento**	moment
el	**reloj**	watch; clock
el	**segundo**	second
el	**siglo**	century
el	**tiempo**	time

USEFUL PHRASES

a mediodía at midday
a medianoche at midnight
pasado mañana the day after tomorrow
hoy today
hoy en día nowadays
anteayer, antes de ayer the day before yesterday
mañana tomorrow
ayer yesterday
hace dos días 2 days ago
dentro de dos días in 2 days
una semana a week
una quincena a fortnight
todos los días every day
¿a qué día estamos?, ¿qué día es hoy? what day is it?
¿cuál es la fecha de hoy? what's the date?
de momento at the moment
las tres menos cuarto a quarter to 3
las tres y cuarto a quarter past 3
en el siglo XXI in the 21st century
ayer por la noche last night, yesterday evening

ESSENTIAL WORDS *(feminine)*

la	**hora**	hour; time *(in general)*
la	**jornada**	day
la	**mañana**	morning
la	**media hora**	half an hour
la	**noche**	night; evening
la	**quincena**	fortnight
la	**semana**	week
la	**tarde**	afternoon; evening

USEFUL PHRASES

el año pasado/próximo last/next year

la semana/el año que viene next week/year

dentro de media hora in half an hour

una vez once

dos/tres veces two/three times

varias veces several times

tres veces al año three times a year

nueve de cada diez veces nine times out of ten

érase una vez once upon a time there was

diez a la vez ten at a time

¿qué hora es? what time is it?

¿tiene hora? have you got the time?

son las seis/las seis menos diez/las seis y media it is 6 o'clock/10 to 6/
    half past 6

son las dos en punto it is 2 o'clock exactly

hace un rato a while ago

dentro de un rato in a while

temprano early

tarde late

esta noche *(past)* last night; *(to come)* tonight

IMPORTANT WORDS *(masculine)*

el **día siguiente**	next day
el **futuro**	future; future tense
el **pasado**	past; past tense
el **presente**	present (*time*); present tense
el **retraso**	delay

USEFUL WORDS *(masculine)*

el **año bisiesto**	leap year
el **calendario**	calendar
el **cronómetro**	stopwatch
el **reloj de pie**	grandfather clock
el **reloj de pulsera**	wristwatch

USEFUL PHRASES

pasado mañana the day after tomorrow
dos días después two days later
el día antes *or* el día anterior the day before
un día sí y otro no every other day
en el futuro in the future
un día libre a day off
un día de fiesta a public holiday
un día laborable a weekday
en un día de lluvia, en un día lluvioso on a rainy day
al amanecer, al alba at dawn
la mañana/tarde siguiente the following morning/evening
ahora now

USEFUL WORDS *(feminine)*

las	**agujas**	hands *(of clock)*
la	**década**	decade
la	**Edad Media**	Middle Ages
la	**época**	time; era
la	**esfera**	face *(of clock)*
las	**manecillas**	hands *(of clock)*

USEFUL PHRASES

llegas tarde you are late
llegas temprano you are early
este reloj adelanta/atrasa this watch is fast/slow
llegar a tiempo, llegar a la hora to arrive on time
¿cuánto tiempo? how long?
el tercer milenio the third millennium
no levantarse hasta tarde to have a lie-in
de un momento a otro any minute now
dentro de una semana in a week's time
el lunes que viene no el otro a week on Monday
la noche antes, la noche anterior the night before
en esa época at that time

ESSENTIAL WORDS *(masculine)*

el	**bricolaje**	DIY
el	**manitas** *(pl inv)*	handyman
el	**taller**	workshop

USEFUL WORDS *(masculine)*

el	**alambre (de espino)**	(barbed) wire
los	**alicates**	pliers
el	**andamio**	scaffolding
el	**candado**	padlock
el	**celo** *(Sp)*	Sellotape®
el	**chinche** *(LAm)*	drawing pin
el	**cincel**	chisel
el	**clavo**	nail
el	**destornillador**	screwdriver
el	**durex®** *(LAm)*	Sellotape®
el	**martillo**	hammer
el	**muelle**	spring
el	**pico**	pickaxe
el	**pincel**	paintbrush
el	**taladro**	drill
el	**tornillo**	screw

USEFUL PHRASES

hacer bricolaje, hacer chapuzas to do odd jobs
clavar un clavo con el martillo to hammer in a nail
"recién pintado(a)" "wet paint"
pintar to paint
empapelar to wallpaper

ESSENTIAL WORDS *(feminine)*

la	cuerda	rope
la	herramienta	tool
la	llave	key; *(LAm)* tap
la	llave inglesa	spanner
la	manitas *(pl inv)*	handywoman
la	máquina	machine

USEFUL WORDS *(feminine)*

la	aguja	needle
la	batería	battery *(in car)*
la	caja de herramientas	toolbox
la	cerradura	lock
la	chinche *(LAm)*	drawing pin
la	chincheta *(Sp)*	drawing pin
la	cola	glue
la	escalera (de mano)	ladder
la	goma (elástica)	rubber band
la	horca	*(garden)* fork
la	lima	file
la	obra	construction site
la	pala	spade
la	pila	battery *(in radio etc)*
la	sierra	saw
la	tabla	plank
la	taladradora	pneumatic drill
las	tijeras	scissors

USEFUL PHRASES

"prohibido el paso a la obra" "construction site: keep out"
práctico(a) handy
cortar to cut
reparar to mend
atornillar to screw (in)
desatornillar to unscrew

ESSENTIAL WORDS (*masculine*)

los	**alrededores**	surroundings
el	**aparcamiento** (*Sp*)	car park; parking space
el	**autobús** (*pl* autobuses)	bus
el	**ayuntamiento**	town hall; town council
el	**banco**	bank; bench
el	**barrio**	district
el	**bloque de departamentos** (*LAm*)	block of flats
el	**bloque de pisos** (*Sp*)	block of flats
el	**café**	café; coffee
el	**carro** (*LAm*)	car
el	**centro de la ciudad**	town centre
el	**cine**	cinema
el	**coche** (*Sp*)	car
el	**edificio**	building
el	**estacionamiento** (*LAm*)	car park; parking space
el	**habitante**	inhabitant
el	**hotel**	hotel
el	**mercado**	market
el	**metro**	underground, subway
el	**museo**	museum; art gallery
el	**parking** (*pl* ~s)	car park
el	**parque**	park
el	**peatón** (*pl* peatones)	pedestrian
el	**policía**	policeman
el	**puente**	bridge
el	**restaurante**	restaurant
el	**suburbio**	suburb; slum area
el	**taxi**	taxi
el	**teatro**	theatre
el	**tour** (*pl* ~s)	tour
el	**turista**	tourist

ESSENTIAL WORDS *(feminine)*

la	**boutique**	boutique
la	**calle**	street
la	**carretera**	road
la	**catedral**	cathedral
la	**ciudad**	town, city
la	**comisaría**	police station
la	**contaminación**	air pollution
la	**esquina**	corner
la	**estación (de trenes)**	(train) station
	(*pl* estaciones (~~))	
la	**estación de autobuses**	bus station
	(*pl* estaciones ~~)	
la	**fábrica**	factory
la	**gasolinera**	petrol station
la	**habitante**	inhabitant
la	**lavandería automática**	launderette
la	**oficina**	office
la	**oficina de correos**	post office
la	**parada de autobús**	bus stop
la	**parada de taxis**	taxi rank
la	**piscina**	swimming pool
la	**plaza**	square
la	**policía**	policewoman; police
la	**tienda**	shop
la	**torre**	tower
la	**turista**	tourist
la	**vista**	view
la	**vivienda de protección oficial**	council flat

USEFUL PHRASES

voy a la ciudad *or* al centro I'm going into town
en el centro (de la ciudad) in the town centre
en la plaza in the square
una calle de sentido único a one-way street
una zona muy urbanizada a built-up area
"dirección prohibida" "no entry"
cruzar la calle to cross the road

IMPORTANT WORDS *(masculine)*

el	abono	season ticket
el	agente (de policía)	police officer
el	alcalde	mayor
el	atasco	traffic jam
el	cartel	notice; poster
el	castillo	castle
el	cibercafé	internet café
el	cruce	crossroads
los	jardines públicos	park
el	lugar	place
el	monumento	monument
el	parquímetro	parking meter
el	quiosco de periódicos	news stand
el	semáforo	traffic lights
el	sitio	place
el	tráfico	traffic
el	transeúnte	passer-by
el	zoológico	zoo

USEFUL PHRASES

en la esquina de la calle at the corner of the street
vivir en las afueras to live in the outskirts
andar, caminar to walk
tomar el autobús/el metro, coger el autobús/el metro (*Sp*) to take the bus/the underground
comprar una tarjeta multiviajes to buy a multiple-journey ticket
picar to punch (*ticket*)

IMPORTANT WORDS *(feminine)*

la	acera	pavement
la	agente (de policía)	police officer
la	alcaldesa	mayor
la	biblioteca	library
la	calle principal	main street
la	calzada	road
la	circulación	traffic
la	desviación *(pl* desviaciones)	diversion
la	estación de servicio	petrol station
	(pl estaciones ~ ~)	
la	iglesia	church
la	máquina expendedora de	ticket machine
	billetes *(Sp) or* de boletos *(LAm)*	
la	mezquita	mosque
la	parte antigua	old town
la	polución	air pollution
la	sinagoga	synagogue
la	tarjeta multiviajes	multiple-journey ticket
la	transeúnte	passer-by
la	zona azul	restricted parking zone
la	zona industrial	industrial estate
la	zona peatonal	pedestrian precinct

USEFUL PHRASES

industrial industrial
histórico(a)historic
bonito(a) pretty
feo(a) ugly
limpio(a)clean
sucio(a) dirty

USEFUL WORDS *(masculine)*

el	adoquín *(pl* adoquines)	cobblestone
el	barrio residencial	residential area
el	callejón sin salida *(pl* callejones ~ ~)	cul-de-sac, dead end
el	camino de bicicletas	cycle path
el	carril bici	cycle lane
el	cementerio	cemetery
el	ciudadano	citizen
el	cochecito (de niño)	pram, buggy
el	concejo municipal	town council
el	desfile	parade
el	distrito	district
el	edificio	building
el	embotellamiento	traffic jam
el	folleto	leaflet
los	lugares de interés	sights, places of interest
el	paradero de autobús *(LAm)*	bus stop
el	parque de bomberos *(Sp)*	fire station
el	paso de cebra	zebra crossing
el	paso de peatones	pedestrian crossing
el	pavimento	road surface
el	rascacielos *(pl inv)*	skyscraper
el	sondeo de opinión	opinion poll

USEFUL WORDS (*feminine*)

las	afueras	outskirts
la	alcantarilla	sewer
la	cafetería	coffee shop, café; canteen
la	calle sin salida	cul-de-sac, dead end
la	camioneta de reparto	delivery van
la	cárcel	prison
la	ciudadana	citizen
la	cola	queue
la	ciudad universitaria	university campus
la	curva	bend
la	estación de bomberos (*pl* estaciones ~ ~) (*LAm*)	fire station
la	estatua	statue
la	farola	street lamp
la	flecha	arrow
la	galería de arte	art gallery
la	isla peatonal	traffic island
la	muchedumbre	crowd
la	multitud	crowd
la	muralla	rampart
la	parada de autobús	bus stop
la	población (*pl* poblaciones)	population
la	señal de tráfico	road sign

ESSENTIAL WORDS *(masculine)*

el	**andén** (*pl* andenes)	platform
el	**asiento**	seat
el	**AVE**	high-speed train
el	**billete** (*Sp*)	ticket
el	**billete de ida** (*Sp*)	single ticket
el	**billete de ida y vuelta** (*Sp*)	return ticket
el	**billete sencillo** (*Sp*)	single ticket
el	**boleto** (*LAm*)	ticket
el	**boleto de ida** (*LAm*)	single ticket
el	**boleto de ida y vuelta** (*LAm*)	return ticket
el	**bolso** (*Sp*)	handbag
el	**compartimento**	compartment
el	**descuento**	reduction
el	**enlace**	connection
el	**equipaje**	luggage
el	**expreso**	fast train
el	**freno**	brake
el	**horario**	timetable
el	**maletero**	porter
el	**metro**	underground, subway
el	**número**	number
el	**oficial de aduanas**	customs officer
el	**pasaporte**	passport
el	**plano**	map
el	**precio del billete** (*Sp*) *or* **del boleto** (*LAm*)	fare
el	**puente**	bridge
el	**recargo**	extra charge
el	**retraso**	delay
el	**taxi**	taxi
el	**tícket** (*pl* ~s)	ticket; receipt
el	**tren**	train
el	**vagón** (*pl* vagones)	carriage
el	**viaje**	journey
el	**viajero**	traveller

ESSENTIAL WORDS (feminine)

la	aduana	customs
la	bici	bike
la	bicicleta	bicycle
la	boletería (LAm)	ticket office
la	bolsa	bag
la	cafetería (de la estación)	station buffet
la	cantina (de la estación)	station buffet
la	cartera	wallet; (LAm) handbag
la	clase	class
la	conexión (pl conexiones)	connection
la	consigna	left-luggage office
la	consigna automática	left-luggage locker
la	dirección (pl direcciones)	direction
la	entrada	entrance
la	estación (pl estaciones)	station
la	estación de metro (pl estaciones ~ ~)	underground station
la	información	information
la	línea	line
la	llegada	arrival
la	maleta	suitcase
la	oficial de aduanas	customs officer
la	oficina de objetos perdidos	lost property office
la	parada de taxis	taxi rank
la	petaca (Mex)	suitcase
la	reserva	reservation
la	sala de espera	waiting room
la	salida	departure; exit
la	taquilla	ticket office; locker
la	vía	track, line
la	viajera	traveller

USEFUL PHRASES

reservar un asiento to book a seat

pagar un recargo, pagar un suplemento to pay an extra charge, to pay a surcharge

hacer/deshacer el equipaje to pack/unpack

IMPORTANT WORDS (*masculine*)

el **coche-cama** (*pl* ~s~)	sleeping car
el **coche-comedor** (*pl* ~s~)	dining car
el **conductor**	driver
el **destino**	destination
el **ferrocarril**	railway
el **revisor**	ticket collector

USEFUL WORDS (*masculine*)

el **abono**	season ticket
el **baúl**	trunk
el **carnet joven** (*pl* ~s ~)	young persons' discount card
el **coche**	carriage
el **descarrilamiento**	derailment
el **jefe de estación**	stationmaster
el **maquinista**	engine-driver
el **panel informativo**	noticeboard
el **paso a nivel**	level crossing
el **silbato**	whistle
el **suplemento**	extra charge, supplement
el **trayecto**	journey
el **(tren de) mercancías** (*pl* (~es ~) ~)	goods train

USEFUL PHRASES

tomar el tren, coger el tren (*Sp*) to take the train
perder el tren to miss the train
montarse en el tren to get on the train
bajar del tren to get off the train
¿está libre este asiento? is this seat free?
el tren lleva retraso the train is late
un vagón de fumadores/no fumadores a smoking/ non-smoking
  compartment
"prohibido asomarse por la ventanilla" "do not lean out of the window"

IMPORTANT WORDS *(feminine)*

la	**barrera**	barrier
la	**conductora**	driver
la	**duración** *(pl* duraciones)	length (of time)
la	**escalera mecánica**	escalator
la	**frontera**	border
la	**litera**	couchette
la	**propina**	tip
la	**RENFE**	Spanish Railway
la	**revisora**	ticket collector
la	**tarifa**	fare

USEFUL WORDS *(feminine)*

la	**alarma**	alarm
la	**etiqueta**	label
la	**jefa de estación**	stationmaster
la	**locomotora**	locomotive
la	**maquinista**	engine-driver
la	**vía férrea**	(railway) line or track
las	**vías**	rails

USEFUL PHRASES

te acompañaré a la estación I'll go to the station with you
iré a buscarte a la estación I'll come and pick you up at the station
el tren de las diez con destino a/procedente de Madrid the 10 o'clock train
  to/from Madrid

ESSENTIAL WORDS (*masculine*)

el	árbol	tree
el	bosque	wood

USEFUL WORDS (*masculine*)

el	abedul	birch
el	abeto	fir tree
el	acebo	holly
el	albaricoque	apricot tree
el	árbol frutal	fruit tree
el	arbusto	bush
el	arce	maple
el	boj	box tree
el	brote	bud
el	castaño	chestnut tree
el	cerezo	cherry tree
el	chabacano (*Mex*)	apricot tree
el	chopo	poplar
el	duraznero (*LAm*)	peach tree
el	espino	hawthorn
el	follaje	foliage
el	fresno	ash
el	huerto	orchard
el	limonero	lemon tree
el	manzano	apple tree
el	melocotonero (*Sp*)	peach tree
el	naranjo	orange tree
el	nogal	walnut tree
el	olmo	elm
el	peral	pear tree
el	pino	pine
el	platanero	banana tree
el	plátano	plane tree
el	roble	oak
el	sauce llorón (*pl* ~s llorones)	weeping willow
el	tejo	yew
el	tilo	lime tree
el	tronco	trunk
el	viñedo	vineyard

ESSENTIAL WORDS *(feminine)*

la	**hoja**	leaf
la	**rama**	branch
la	**selva (tropical)**	rain forest

USEFUL WORDS *(feminine)*

la	**baya**	berry
la	**corteza**	bark
la	**encina**	ilex, holm oak
el	**haya** (*pl f* las hayas)	beech
la	**higuera**	fig tree
la	**raíz** (*pl* raíces)	root
la	**viña**	vineyard

ESSENTIAL WORDS *(masculine)*

el	**ajo**	garlic
los	**champiñones**	mushrooms
los	**chícharos** *(Mex)*	peas
los	**ejotes** *(Mex)*	French beans
los	**guisantes** *(Sp)*	peas
el	**pimiento**	pepper
el	**tomate**	tomato

USEFUL WORDS *(masculine)*

el	**apio**	celery
el	**berro**	watercress
el	**brécol**	broccoli
el	**calabacín** *(pl* calabacines)	courgette
el	**elote** *(Mex)*	sweetcorn
los	**espárragos**	asparagus
los	**frijoles** *(LAm)*	beans
los	**garbanzos**	chickpeas
el	**maíz (dulce** *or* **tierno)**	sweetcorn
el	**nabo**	turnip
el	**pepino**	cucumber
el	**perejil**	parsley
el	**pimiento morrón** *(pl* ~s morrones)	(sweet) pepper
el	**puerro**	leek
el	**rábano**	radish
el	**repollo**	cabbage

USEFUL PHRASES

cultivar verduras to grow vegetables
una mazorca de maíz *(Sp)*, una mazorca de choclo *(Mex)* corn on the cob

ESSENTIAL WORDS *(feminine)*

las	**arvejas** *(LAm)*	peas
la	**cebolla**	onion
la	**coliflor**	cauliflower
la	**ensalada**	salad
las	**habichuelas** *(LAm)*	French beans
las	**judías verdes** *(Sp)*	French beans
la	**papa** *(LAm, Southern Sp)*,	potato
la	**patata** *(Sp)*	
las	**verduras**	vegetables
la	**zanahoria**	carrot

USESFUL WORDS *(feminine)*

la	**alcachofa**	artichoke
las	**alubias** *(Sp)*	beans
la	**berenjena**	aubergine
la	**calabacita** *(Mex)*	courgette
la	**calabaza**	pumpkin
la	**cebolleta**	spring onion
la	**col**	cabbage
las	**coles de Bruselas**	Brussels sprouts
la	**endibia**	endive, chicory
la	**escarola**	curly endive
las	**espinacas**	spinach
las	**judías**	beans
las	**judías blancas**	haricot beans
la	**lechuga**	lettuce
las	**legumbres**	pulses
las	**lentejas**	lentils
la	**remolacha**	beetroot

USEFUL PHRASES

zanahoria rallada **grated carrot**
biológico(a) **organic**
vegetariano(a) **vegetarian**

ESSENTIAL WORDS *(masculine)*

el	**autobús** (*pl* autobuses)	bus
el	**autocar**	coach
el	**avión** (*pl* aviones)	plane
el	**barco de vela**	sailing ship; sailing boat
el	**bote**	boat
el	**bote de remos**	rowing boat
el	**camión** (*pl* camiones)	lorry
el	**carro**	cart; (*LAm*) car
el	**casco**	helmet
el	**ciclomotor**	moped
el	**coche** (*Sp*)	car
el	**coche de línea**	coach
el	**helicóptero**	helicopter
el	**medio de transporte**	means of transport
el	**metro**	underground, subway
el	**precio del billete** (*Sp*) *or* del boleto (*LAm*)	fare
el	**taxi**	taxi
el	**transbordador**	ferry
el	**transporte público**	public transport
el	**tren**	train
el	**vehículo**	vehicle
el	**vehículo pesado**	heavy goods vehicle

USEFUL PHRASES

viajar to travel

ha ido a Barcelona en avión **he flew to Barcelona**

tomar el autobús/el metro/el tren, coger (*Sp*) el autobús/el metro/el tren to take the bus/the subway/the train

montar en bicicleta **to go cycling**

se puede ir en coche **you can go there by car**

ESSENTIAL WORDS *(feminine)*

la	**bici**	bike
la	**bicicleta**	bicycle
la	**camioneta**	van
la	**caravana**	caravan
la	**distancia**	distance
la	**moto**	motorbike
la	**motocicleta**	motorcycle, motorbike
la	**parte de atrás**	back
la	**parte de delante**	front
la	**parte delantera**	front
la	**parte trasera**	back
la	**vespa**®	scooter

IMPORTANT WORDS *(masculine)*

el	**coche de bomberos**	fire engine

IMPORTANT WORDS *(feminine)*

la	**ambulancia**	ambulance
la	**grúa**	breakdown van

USEFUL PHRASES

reparar el coche de algn to repair sb's car
un coche de alquiler a hire car
un coche deportivo a sports car
un coche de carreras a racing car
un coche de empresa a company car
"coches de ocasión" "used cars"
arrancar to start, to move off

USEFUL WORDS *(masculine)*

el	**aerodeslizador**	hovercraft
el	**(barco de) vapor**	steamer
el	**bulldozer** *(pl ~s)*	bulldozer
el	**buque**	ship
el	**camión articulado** *(pl camiones ~s)*	articulated lorry
el	**camión cisterna** *(pl camiones ~)*	tanker
el	**cochecito (de niño)**	pram, buggy
el	**cohete**	rocket
el	**hidroavión** *(pl hidroaviones)*	seaplane
el	**jeep** *(pl ~s)*	jeep
el	**navío**	ship
el	**ovni (objeto volante no identificado)**	UFO *(unidentified flying object)*
el	**petrolero**	oil tanker *(ship)*
el	**planeador**	glider
el	**platillo volante**	flying saucer
el	**portaaviones** *(pl inv)*	aircraft carrier
el	**remolcador**	tug
el	**remolque**	trailer
el	**riesgo**	risk
el	**submarino**	submarine
el	**tanque**	tank
el	**teleférico**	cable car
el	**telesilla**	chairlift
el	**tranvía**	tram
el	**velero**	sailing ship; sailing boat
el	**velomotor**	moped
el	**yate**	yacht; pleasure cruiser

USEFUL WORDS *(feminine)*

la	barcaza	barge
la	camioneta de reparto	delivery van
la	canoa	canoe
la	carreta	waggon; cart
la	golondrina	pleasure boat
la	lancha	boat (*small*); launch
la	lancha de salvamento	lifeboat
la	lancha de socorro	lifeboat
la	lancha neumática	rubber dinghy
la	lancha rápida	speedboat
la	locomotora	locomotive
la	ranchera	estate car

ESSENTIAL WORDS (*masculine*)

el	**aire**	air
el	**boletín meteorológico** (*pl* boletines ~s)	weather report
el	**calor**	heat
el	**cielo**	sky
el	**clima**	climate
el	**este**	east
el	**frío**	cold
el	**grado**	degree
el	**hielo**	ice
el	**invierno**	winter
el	**norte**	north
el	**oeste**	west
el	**otoño**	autumn
el	**paraguas** (*pl inv*)	umbrella
el	**parte meteorológico**	weather report
el	**pronóstico del tiempo**	(weather) forecast
el	**sol**	sun; sunshine
el	**sur**	south
el	**tiempo**	weather
el	**verano**	summer
el	**viento**	wind

USEFUL PHRASES

¿qué tiempo hace? what's the weather like?

hace calor/frío it's hot/cold

hace un día estupendo, hace un día precioso it's a lovely day

hace un día horrible it's a horrible day

al aire libre in the open air

hay niebla it's foggy

30° a la sombra 30° in the shade

escuchar el pronóstico del tiempo to listen to the weather forecast

llover to rain

nevar to snow

llueve it's raining

nieva it's snowing

ESSENTIAL WORDS *(feminine)*

la	**estación** *(pl* estaciones)	season
la	**lluvia**	rain
la	**niebla**	fog
la	**nieve**	snow
la	**nube**	cloud
la	**primavera**	spring
la	**región** *(pl* regiones)	region, area
la	**temperatura**	temperature

USEFUL PHRASES

brilla el sol the sun is shining

sopla el viento the wind is blowing

hace un frío que pela it's freezing

helarse to freeze

ha helado there's been a frost

fundirse to melt

soleado(a) sunny

tormentoso(a) stormy

lluvioso(a) rainy

frío(a) cool

variable changeable

húmedo(a) humid

el cielo está cubierto the sky is overcast

IMPORTANT WORDS *(masculine)*

el **chaparrón** *(pl* chaparrones)	shower
el **claro**	sunny spell
el **humo**	smoke
el **polvo**	dust

USEFUL WORDS *(masculine)*

el **aguacero**	downpour
el **amanecer**	dawn, daybreak
el **anochecer**	nightfall, dusk
el **arco iris** *(pl inv)*	rainbow
el **barómetro**	barometer
el **cambio**	change
el **carámbano**	icicle
el **charco**	puddle
el **copo de nieve**	snowflake
el **crepúsculo**	twilight
el **deshielo**	thaw
el **granizo**	hail
el **huracán** *(pl* huracanes)	hurricane
el **pararrayos** *(pl inv)*	lightning conductor
el **quitanieves** *(pl inv)*	snowplough
el **rayo**	lightning
el **rayo de sol**	ray of sunshine
el **relámpago**	flash of lightning
el **rocío**	dew
el **trueno**	thunder

IMPORTANT WORDS (feminine)

las	precipitaciones	rainfall
la	previsión meteorológica	(weather) forecast
	(pl previsiones ~s)	
la	sombrilla	parasol
la	tormenta	storm
la	visibilidad	visibility

USEFUL WORDS (feminine)

el	alba (pl f las albas)	dawn
la	atmósfera	atmosphere
la	brisa	breeze
la	bruma	mist
la	corriente (de aire)	draught
la	escarcha	frost (on the ground)
la	gota de lluvia	raindrop
la	helada	frost (weather)
la	inundación (pl inundaciones)	flood
la	luz de la luna	moonlight
la	mejora	improvement
la	nevada	snowfall
la	ola de calor	heatwave
la	oscuridad	darkness
la	puesta de sol	sunset
la	ráfaga de viento	gust of wind
la	sequía	drought
la	tormenta	thunderstorm
la	ventisca	snowdrift

ESSENTIAL WORDS *(masculine)*

el	albergue juvenil	youth hostel
los	baños públicos *(LAm)*	toilets
el	bote de la basura *(Mex)*	dustbin
el	comedor	dining room
el	cuarto de baño	bathroom
el	cubo de la basura	dustbin
el	desayuno	breakfast
el	dormitorio	dormitory
los	lavabos	toilets
el	mapa	map
los	servicios *(Sp)*	toilets
el	silencio	silence
el	visitante	visitor

IMPORTANT WORDS *(masculine)*

el	carnet de socio *(pl ~s ~~)*	membership card
el	lavabo	washbasin; toilet
el	saco de dormir	sleeping bag

ESSENTIAL WORDS *(feminine)*

la	cama	bed
la	(cama) litera	bunk bed
la	cocina	kitchen; cooking
la	comida	meal
la	ducha	shower
la	estancia	stay
la	lista de precios	price list
la	noche	night
la	oficina	office
la	sábana	sheet
la	sala de juegos	games room
la	tarifa	rate(s)
las	vacaciones	holidays
la	visitante	visitor

IMPORTANT WORDS *(feminine)*

la	caminata	hike
la	excursión (*pl* excursiones)	trip
la	guía	guidebook
la	mochila	rucksack
las	normas	rules
la	ropa de cama	bed linen

USEFUL PHRASES

pasar una noche en el albergue juvenil to spend a night at the youth hostel

quisiera alquilar un saco de dormir I would like to hire a sleeping bag

está todo ocupado there's no more room

The vocabulary items on pages 204 to 233 have been grouped under parts of speech rather than topics because they can apply in a wide range of circumstances. Use them just as freely as the vocabulary already given.

ARTICLES AND PRONOUNS

What is an article?
In English, an **article** is one of the words *the*, *a* and *an* which is given in front of a noun.

What is a pronoun?
A **pronoun** is a word you use instead of a noun, when you do not need or want to name someone or something directly, for example, *it*, *you*, *none*.

algo something; anything
alguien somebody, someone; anybody, anyone
alguno/alguna one; someone, somebody
algunos/algunas some, some of them; some of us, some of you, some of them
ambos/ambas both
aquel/aquella; aquél/aquélla that
aquellos/aquellas; aquéllos/aquéllas those
cada each; every
cual which; who; whom
  lo cual which
cuál what, which one
cualquiera any one; anybody, anyone
  cualquiera de los dos/las dos either (*see also* Adjectives)
cualesquiera (*pl*) any (*see also* Adjectives)
cuanto/cuanta as much as
cuánto/cuánta how much
cuantos/cuantas as many as
cuántos/cuántas how many
cuyo/cuya/cuyos/cuyas whose

  en cuyo caso in which case
demasiado/demasiada too much
demasiados too many
dos: los/las dos both
el/la the
él he; him; it
  de él his
ella she; her; it
  de ella hers
ello it
ellos/ellas they; them
  de ellos/ellas theirs
ese/esa; ése/ésa that
esos/esas; ésos/ésas those
este/esta; éste/ésta this
estos/estas; éstos/éstas these
la her; it; you
las them; you
le him; her; it; you
les them; you
lo him; it; you
los/las the
los them; you
me me; myself
mi/mis my
(el)mío/(la) mía/(los) míos/(las) mías mine

mismo/misma/mismos/mismas same
  mí mismo/misma; yo mismo/misma myself; **nosotros mismos/nosotras mismas** ourselves; **sí misma; ella misma** herself; **sí mismo; él mismo** himself; **sí mismos/sí mismas; ellos mismos/ellas mismas** themselves; **ti mismo/ti misma; tú mismo/tú misma; usted mismo/usted misma** yourself; **vosotros mismos/vosotras mismas; ustedes mismos/ustedes mismas** yourselves; **uno mismo/una misma** oneself
mucho/mucha a lot, lots; much (see also Adjectives; Adverbs)
muchos/muchas a lot, lots; many (see also Adjectives)
nada nothing
  nada más nothing else
nadie nobody, no one; anybody, anyone
  nadie más nobody else
ninguno/ninguna any; neither; either; none; no one, nobody
  ninguno de los dos/ninguna de las dos neither (see also Adjectives)
ningunos/ningunas any; none (see also Adjectives)
nos us; ourselves; each other
nosotros/nosotras we; us
nuestro/nuestra/nuestros/nuestras our; ours
  el nuestro/la nuestra/los nuestros/las nuestras ours
os you; yourselves; each other
otro/otra another, another one (see also Adjectives)

otros/otras others (see also Adjectives)
poco/poca un poco a bit, a little
  dentro de poco shortly
pocos/pocas not many, few
que who; that
qué what; what a
quien/quienes who; whoever
quién/quiénes who
se him; her; them; you; himself; herself; itself; themselves; yourself; yourselves; oneself; each other
su/sus his; her; its; their; your; one's
(el) suyo/(la) suya /(los) suyos/(las) suyas his; her; its; their; your; hers; theirs; yours; one's own
tal/tales such
tampoco not...either, neither
te you; yourself
ti you
todo/toda (it) all
  todo el mundo everybody, everyone (see also Adjectives)
todos/todas all; every; everybody; everyone (see also Adjectives)
tu/tus your
tú you
usted you
ustedes you
(el) tuyo/ (la) tuya/ (los) tuyos/(las) tuyas yours
un/una a; an; one
unos/unas some; a few; about, around
varios/varias several
vosotros/vosotras you
vuestro/vuestra/vuestros/vuestras your; yours
  los vuestros/las vuestras yours
yo I; me

CONJUNCTIONS

> **What is a conjunction?**
> A **conjunction** is a word such as *and*, *but*, *or*, *so*, *if* and *because*, that links two words or phrases of a similar type, or two parts of a sentence, for example, *Diane* <u>and</u> *I have been friends for years*; *I left* <u>because</u> *I was bored*.

ahora though
  ahora bien however; **ahora que** now that
antes: antes de que before
así: así (es) que so
  así pues so
aunque although, though
como as
conque so, so then
consiguiente: por consiguiente so, therefore
cuando when; whenever; if
cuanto: en cuanto as soon as; as
dar: dado que since
decir: es decir that is to say
desde: desde que since
después: después de que after
e and
embargo: sin embargo still, however
entonces then
fin: a fin de que so that, in order that
forma: de forma que so that
hasta: hasta que until, till
luego therefore
manera: de manera que so that
mas but
más: más que more than
menos: menos que less than
mientras while; as long as
  mientras que whereas; **mientras (tanto)** meanwhile
modo: de modo que so that
momento: en el momento en que just as
ni or; nor; even
  ni...ni neither...nor
o or
  o ... o ... either ... or ...
para: para que so that
pero but
porque because
pronto: tan pronto como as soon as
pues then; well; since
puesto: puesto que since
que that
ser: o sea that is
  a no ser que unless
si if; whether
  si no otherwise
siempre: siempre que whenever; as long as, provided that
sino but; except; only
tal: con tal (de) que as long as, provided that
tanto: por (lo) tanto so, therefore
u or
vez: una vez que once
vista: en vista de que seeing that
y and
ya: ya que as, since

ADJECTIVES

> **What is an adjective?**
> An **adjective** is a 'describing' word that tells you more about a person or thing, such as their appearance, colour, size or other qualities, for example, *pretty*, *blue*, *big*.

abierto(a) open
absoluto(a) absolute
absurdo(a) absurd
académico(a) academic
accesible accessible; approachable
aceptable acceptable
acondicionado(a) fitted out
  con aire acondicionado
  air-conditioned
acostumbrado(a) accustomed
activo(a) active
acusado(a) accused; marked
adecuado(a) appropriate
admirable admirable
aéreo(a) aerial
afilado(a) sharp
afortunado(a) fortunate, lucky
agitado(a) rough; agitated; hectic
agotado(a) exhausted
agradable pleasant, agreeable
agresivo(a) aggressive
agrícola agricultural
aficionado(a) keen
agudo(a) sharp; acute
aislado(a) isolated
alegre happy; bright; lively; merry
alguno/alguna (*before masc sing*
  algún) some; any (*see also* Articles
  and Pronouns)
algunos/algunas some; several
  (*see also* Articles and Pronouns)
alternativo(a) alternating; alternative

alto(a) high; tall
amargo(a) bitter
ancho(a) broad; wide
anciano(a) elderly
animado(a) lively; cheerful
anónimo(a) anonymous
anormal abnormal
anterior former
antiguo(a) old; vintage; antique
anual annual
apagado(a) out; off; muffled; dull
aparente apparent
apasionado(a) passionate
apropiado(a) appropriate, suitable
aproximado(a) rough
arriba: de arriba top
asequible affordable
asombrado(a) amazed, astonished
asombroso(a) amazing,
  astonishing
áspero(a) rough
atestado(a) crowded; popular
atento(a) attentive; watchful
atractivo(a) attractive
automático(a) automatic
avanzado(a) advanced
bajo(a) low; short
barba: con barba bearded
barbudo(a) bearded
básico(a) basic
bastante enough; quite a lot of
  (*see also* Adverbs)

bien well-to-do
bienvenido(a) welcome
blando(a) soft
breve brief
brillante shining; bright
brutal brutal
bruto(a) rough; stupid; uncouth; gross
bueno(a) good
cada each; every
caliente hot; warm
callado(a) quiet
cansado(a) tired
capaz capable
cariñoso(a) affectionate
caro(a) expensive, dear
cauteloso(a) cautious
central central
ceñido(a) tight
cercano(a) close; nearby
cerrado(a) closed; off
científico(a) scientific
cierto(a) true; certain
civil civil; civilian
claro(a) clear; light; bright
clásico(a) classical; classic
climatizado(a) air-conditioned
cobarde cowardly
comercial commercial
cómodo(a) comfortable
complejo(a) complex
completo(a) complete
complicado(a) complicated; complex
comprensivo(a) understanding
común common; mutual
concreto(a) specific; concrete
concurrido(a) crowded; popular
conmovedor(a) moving
consciente conscious; aware

conservador(a) conservative
considerable considerable
constante constant
contemporáneo(a) contemporary
contento(a) happy; pleased
continuo(a) continuous
convencional conventional
correcto(a) correct, right
corriente ordinary; common
cortado(a) cut; closed; off; shy
creativo(a) creative
cristiano(a) Christian
crítico(a) critical
crudo(a) raw
cuadrado(a) square
cualquiera (*before masc and fem sing* **cualquier)** any (*see also* Articles and Pronouns)
cualesquiera any (*see also* Articles and Pronouns)
cuanto/cuanta as much as
cuánto/cuánta how much
cuantos/cuantas as many as
cuántos/cuántas how many
cultural cultural
curioso(a) curious
debido(a) due, proper
decepcionante disappointing
decidido(a) determined
delicado(a) delicate
delicioso(a) delicious
demasiado/demasiada too much
demasiados too many
democrático(a) democratic
derecho(a) right
desafortunado(a) unfortunate
desagradable unpleasant
desconocido(a) unknown
desesperado(a) desperate

desierto(a) deserted
desnudo(a) naked; bare
despejado(a) clear
despierto(a) awake; sharp; alert
despreocupado(a) carefree; careless
destruido(a) destroyed
detallado(a) detailed
diestro(a) skilful
difícil difficult
digno(a) worthy; dignified
diminuto(a) tiny
directo(a) direct
disgustado(a) upset
disponible available
dispuesto(a) arranged; willing
distinguido(a) distinguished
distinto(a) different; various
divertido(a) funny, amusing; fun;
  entertaining
dividido(a) divided
divino(a) divine
doble double
domesticado(a) tame
doméstico(a) domestic
dos: los/las dos both
dulce sweet
duro(a) hard
económico(a) economic; economical
efectivo(a) effective
eficaz effective; efficient
eficiente efficient
eléctrico(a) electric
electrónico(a) electronic
elemental elementary
emocionante exciting
emotivo(a) emotional; moving
encantador(a) charming; lovely
enmascarado(a) masked
enorme enormous, huge

enterado(a) knowledgeable;
  well-informed; aware
entero(a) whole
equivalente equivalent
equivocado(a) wrong
escandaloso(a) shocking
esencial essential
especial special
específico(a) specific
espectacular spectacular
espeso(a) thick
espiritual spiritual
estrecho(a) narrow
estricto(a) strict
estropeado(a) broken (off); off
estupendo(a) marvellous, great
estúpido(a) stupid
étnico(a) ethnic
evidente obvious, evident
exacto(a) exact; accurate
excelente excellent
excepcional outstanding
exclusivo(a) exclusive
exigente demanding, exacting
experto(a) experienced
éxito: de éxito successful
exitoso(a) successful
exquisito(a) delicious; exquisite
extra extra; top-quality
extranjero(a) foreign
extraño(a) strange; foreign
extraordinario(a) extraordinary;
  outstanding; special
extremo(a) extreme
fácil easy
falso(a) false
familiar family; familiar
famoso(a) famous
fatigoso(a) tiring

federal federal
feroz fierce
fijo(a) fixed; permanent
final final
financiero(a) financial
fino(a) fine; smooth; refined
firme firm; steady
físico(a) physical
flexible flexible
fluido(a) fluid; fluent
formal reliable; formal; official
frágil fragile; frail
frecuente frequent
fresco(a) fresh; cool; cheeky
fuerte strong; loud
futuro(a) future
general general
generoso(a) generous
genial brilliant; wonderful
gentil kind
genuino(a) genuine
global global
gordo(a) fat; big
grande (*before masc sing* gran) big;
  great
grandioso(a) grand; grandiose
habitual usual
herido(a) injured; wounded; hurt
hermoso(a) beautiful
histórico(a) historic; historical
holgado(a) loose
honrado(a) honest; respectable
horrible horrific; hideous; terrible
horroroso(a) dreadful; hideous;
  terrible
humano(a) human; humane
ideal ideal
idéntico(a) identical
igual equal

ilegal illegal
iluminado(a) illuminated, lit;
  enlightened
ilustrado(a) illustrated
imaginario(a) imaginary
impar odd
importante important
imposible impossible
imprescindible indispensable
impresionante impressive;
  moving; shocking
inaguantable unbearable
incapaz (de) incapable (of)
increíble incredible; unbelievable
inculto(a) uncultured
indefenso(a) defenceless
independiente independent
indiferente unconcerned
individual individual; single
industrial industrial
inesperado(a) unexpected
inevitable inevitable
infantil childlike; childish
inflable inflatable
injusto(a) unfair
inmediato(a) immediate
inmenso(a) immense
inmune immune
inquieto(a) anxious; restless
intacto(a) intact
intencionado(a) deliberate
intenso(a) intense; intensive
interior interior; inside; inner;
  domestic
interminable endless
internacional international
interno(a) internal
interrumpido(a) interrupted
inútil useless

invisible invisible
izquierdo(a) left
junto(a) together
justo(a) just, fair; exact; tight
largo(a) long
legal legal
lento(a) slow
libre free
ligero(a) light; slight; agile
limpio(a) clean
liso(a) smooth; straight; plain
listo(a) ready; bright
llamativo(a) bright; striking
llano(a) flat; straightforward
lleno(a) (de) full (of)
lluvioso(a) rainy, wet
loco(a) mad, crazy
lujo: de lujo luxurious
lujoso(a) luxurious
magnífico(a) magnificent;
   wonderful, superb
maligno(a) malignant; evil, malicious
malo(a) bad
malvado(a) wicked
manso(a) meek; tame
maravilloso(a) marvellous,
   wonderful; magic
marcado(a) marked
más more of a
máximo(a) maximum
mayor bigger; elder
   el/la...mayor the biggest...;
   the eldest...
mecánico(a) mechanical
médico(a) medical
medio(a) half; average
medioambiental environmental
mejor better
   el/la mejor the best

menor smaller; younger
   el/la...menor the smallest;
   the youngest
menos less of a
mental mental
militar military
minucioso(a) thorough; very
   detailed
mismo(a) same
misterioso(a) mysterious
moderado(a) moderate
moderno(a) modern
mojado(a) wet; soaked
molesto(a) annoying; annoyed;
   awkward; uncomfortable
montañoso(a) mountainous
mucho/mucha a lot of, lots of;
   much (see also Pronouns; Adverbs)
muchos/muchas a lot of, lots of;
   many (see also Pronouns)
muerto(a) dead
mundial worldwide, global
mutuo(a) mutual
nacido(a) born
nacional national; domestic
nativo(a) native
natural natural
necesario(a) necessary
negativo(a) negative
ninguno/ninguna (before masc sing
   ningún) no; any (see also
   Pronouns)
ningunos/ningunas no; any
   (see also Pronouns)
normal normal; standard
nuclear nuclear
nuevo(a) new
numeroso(a) numerous
obediente obedient

objetivo(a) objective
obligatorio(a) compulsory, obligatory
obvio(a) obvious
ocupado(a) busy; taken; engaged; occupied
oficial official
oportuno(a) opportune; appropriate
original original
oscuro(a) dark; obscure
otro/otra another
  a/en otro lugar somewhere else; **otra cosa** something else; **otra persona** somebody else; **otra vez** again (*see also* Pronouns); **otros/otras** other (*see also* Pronouns)
pacífico(a) peaceful; peaceable
pálido(a) pale
par even
particular special; particular; private
patético(a) pathetic
peligroso(a) dangerous
peor worse
  el peor the worst
perdido(a) lost; stray; remote
perfecto(a) perfect
personal personal
pesado(a) heavy; tedious
picante hot
pie: de pie standing (up)
poco/poca not much, little
pocos/pocas not many, few
poderoso(a) powerful
polémico(a) controversial
polvoriento(a) dusty; powdery
popular popular
portátil portable
posible possible; potential

positivo(a) positive
práctico(a) practical
precioso(a) lovely, beautiful; precious
preciso(a) precise; necessary
preferido(a) favourite
preliminar preliminary
presentable presentable
presunto(a) alleged
previo(a) previous
primario(a) primary
principal main
privado(a) private
privilegiado(a) privileged
profundo(a) deep
prometido(a) promised; engaged
propio(a) own
próximo(a) near, close; next
psicológico(a) psychological
público(a) public
pueril childish
pulcro(a) neat
puntiagudo(a) pointed; sharp
puntual punctual
puro(a) pure
qué what; which; what a
querido(a) dear
químico(a) chemical
racial racial
radical radical
rápido(a) fast, quick
raro(a) strange, odd; rare
razonable reasonable
reacio(a) reluctant
real actual; royal
reciente recent
recto(a) straight; honest
redondo(a) round
refrescante refreshing

regional regional
regular regular
religioso(a) religious
repentino(a) sudden
repuesto: de repuesto spare
reservado(a) reserved
resistente resistant; tough
responsable (de) responsible (for)
revolucionario(a) revolutionary
ridículo(a) ridiculous
rival rival
romántico(a) romantic
rubio(a) fair, blond
ruidoso(a) noisy
rural rural
sabio(a) wise
sagrado(a) sacred
salvaje wild
salvo: a salvo safe
sanitario(a) sanitary; health
sano(a) healthy
   sano(a) y salvo(a) safe and sound
santo(a) holy
satisfecho(a) (de) satisfied (with)
seco(a) dry
secreto(a) secret
secundario(a) secondary
seguro(a) safe; secure; certain; sure
semejante similar
sencillo(a) simple; natural; single
sensacional sensational
sentado(a) sitting, seated
señalado(a) special
separado(a) separate
servicial helpful
severo(a) severe
sexual sexual
significativo(a) significant;
   meaningful

siguiente next, following
silencioso(a) silent; quiet
sincero(a) sincere
singular singular; outstanding
siniestro(a) sinister
situado(a) situated
sobra: de sobra spare
sobrante spare
social social
solemne solemn
sólido(a) solid
solo(a) alone; lonely; black;
   straight, neat
soltero(a) single
sombrío(a) sombre; dim
sonriente smiling
soportable bearable
sorprendente surprising
sospechoso(a) suspicious
suave smooth; gentle; mild; slight
sucio(a) dirty
superior top; upper; superior
supremo(a) supreme
supuesto(a) assumed; supposed
tal/tales such
tanto/tanta so much
tantos/tantas so many
técnico(a) technical
terrible terrible
típico(a) typical
tirante tight; tense
todo/toda all (see also Pronouns)
todos/todas all; every (see also
   Pronouns)
tolerante broad-minded
total total
tradicional traditional
tremendo(a) tremendous
triste sad

último(a) last
  el último the latest
ultrajante offensive; outrageous
único(a) only; unique
urgente urgent
útil useful, helpful
vacante vacant
vacío(a) empty
valiente brave, ourageous
valioso(a) valuable
valor: de valor valuable
variado(a) varied

varios/varias several
vecino(a) neighbouring
verdad: de verdad real
verdadero(a) real; true
viejo(a) old
vil villainous; vile
violento(a) violent; awkward
visible visible
vital vital
vivo(a) living; alive; lively
voluntario(a) voluntary

ADVERBS AND PREPOSITIONS

What is an adverb?
An **adverb** is a word usually used with verbs, adjectives or other adverbs that gives more information about when, how, where, or in what circumstances something happens, or to what degree something is true, for example, *quickly*, *happily*, *now*, *extremely*, *very*.

What is a preposition?
A **preposition** is a word such as *at*, *for*, *with*, *into* or *from*, which is usually followed by a noun, pronoun, or, in English, a word ending in -ing. Prepositions show how people or things relate to the rest of the sentence, for example, *She's at home*; *a tool for cutting grass*; *It's from David*.

a to; at; into: onto
abajo down; downstairs; below
  allá abajo down there
absolutamente absolutely
acá here, over here; now
acerca: acerca de about
actualmente at present
acuerdo: de acuerdo OK, okay
adelante forward
  en adelante from now on
  hacia adelante forward
además also; furthermore, moreover, in addition
  además de as well as; besides
admirablemente admirably
afortunadamente fortunately
agradablemente nicely
ahora now; in a minute
  hasta ahora so far
alcance: al alcance within reach
allá there, over there
allí there
alrededor de around
ansiosamente anxiously
ante before; in the face of; faced with

ante todo above all
antemano: de antemano beforehand, in advance
anteriormente previously, before
antes before **antes de** before
  cuanto antes as soon as possible
  lo antes posible as soon as possible
apartado: apartado de away from
aparte: aparte de apart from
apenas hardly, scarcely; only
aproximadamente approximately
aquí here; now
arriba up; upstairs; above
  allá arriba up there
así like that; like this
  así como as well as
atentamente attentively, carefully; kindly
atrás behind; at the back; backwards; ago
  hacia atrás backwards
aun even **aun así** even so
  aun cuando even if
aún still, yet; even
azar: al azar at random

bajo low; quietly; under
básicamente basically
bastante enough; quite a lot; quite
  (*see also* Adjectives)
bien well; carefully; very; easily
brevemente briefly
bruscamente abruptly
cambio: a cambio de in exchange
  for; in return for
  en cambio instead
camino: de camino on the way
casi almost, nearly
caso: en el caso de (que) in the case of
  en todo caso in any case
casualidad: por casualidad by
  chance
causa: a causa de because of
cerca (de) close (to); near (to)
claramente clearly
cómo how
como like; such as; as; about
completamente completely
con with
concreto: en concreto specifically,
  in particular
continuamente constantly
contra against
correctamente correctly
cortésmente politely
cuando when
cuándo when
cuanto: en cuanto a as regards, as for
cuánto how much; how far; how
cuenta: a fin de cuentas ultimately
  teniendo en cuenta considering
cuidado: con cuidado carefully
cuidadosamente carefully
curiosamente curiously
curso: en el curso de in the course of

de of; from; about; by; than; in; if
debajo underneath
  debajo de under; **por debajo**
  underneath; **por debajo de** under;
  below
débilmente faintly; weakly
delante in front; at the front;
  opposite
  delante de in front of; opposite
  hacia delante forward
  por delante ahead; at the front
demasiado too; too much
dentro inside
  dentro de inside; in; within
deprisa quickly, hurriedly
derecha: a la derecha on the right
desde from; since
desgraciadamente unfortunately
despacio slowly
después later; after(wards); then
  después de after
detrás behind; at the back; on the
  back; after
  detrás de behind; **por detrás** from
  behind; on the back
día: al día per day
diariamente on a daily basis
diario: a diario daily
donde where; wherever
dónde where
dondequiera anywhere
duda: sin duda definitely,
  undoubtedly
dulcemente sweetly; gently
durante during; for
  durante todo/toda throughout
efecto: en efecto in fact
ejemplo: por ejemplo for example
en in; on; at; into; by

encima on top
   encima de above; on top of; **por
   encima** over; **por encima de** over;
   above
enfrente (de) opposite
enseguida right away
entonces then
   desde entonces since then; **hasta
   entonces** until then
entre among(st); between
especialmente especially,
   particularly; specially
evidentemente obviously, evidently
exactamente exactly
excepción: con la excepción de
   with the exception of
excepto except (for)
extranjero: en el extranjero
   overseas; abroad
extremadamente extremely
fácilmente easily
fielmente faithfully
fin: por fin finally; at last
finalmente eventually
forma: de alguna forma somehow
   de esta forma like that; like this;
   de ninguna forma in no way;
   de otra forma otherwise;
   de todas formas anyway
francamente frankly; really
frecuentemente frequently
frente: frente a opposite, facing;
   against
fuera outside; out
   fuera de outside
gana: de buena gana willingly,
   happily
   de mala gana reluctantly
general: por lo general as a rule

generalmente generally
gracias: gracias a thanks to
gradualmente gradually
hacia towards
hasta to, as far as; up to; down to;
   until
honradamente honestly
igualmente equally; likewise
incluido including
inmediatamente immediately
intensamente intensely
izquierda: a la izquierda on the left
jamás never; ever
junto: junto a close to, near; next
   to; together with
   junto con together with
justamente just; exactly; justly
lado: al lado (de) next door (to); near
   al lado de alongside; al otro lado de
   across; de un lado a otro to and fro;
   por este lado (de) on this side (of)
largo: a lo largo de along
lejos (de) far (from)
ligeramente lightly; slightly
luego then; later, afterwards
   desde luego certainly
mal badly; poorly; ill
manera: de alguna manera
   somehow
   de esta manera like that; like this;
   de ninguna manera in no way; de
   otra manera otherwise; de todas
   maneras anyway
más more; plus
   el/la más the most; más allá de
   beyond; más bien rather; más
   cerca closer; más lejos further;
   más o menos about; más...que
   more...than; no más no more

medio: en medio de in the middle of
  por medio de by means of
mejor better
  el mejor the best
menos less; minus
  el/la menos the least;
  menos...que less than; **por lo
  menos** at least
mentalmente mentally
menudo: a menudo often
misteriosamente mysteriously
modo: de algún modo somehow
  de este modo like that; like this;
  de ningún modo in no way; **de
  otro modo** otherwise; **de todos
  modos** anyway
momento: en este momento at
  the moment
  en ese mismo momento at that
  very moment
mucho a lot
  no mucho not much (*see also*
  Pronouns; Adjectives)
muy very
naturalmente naturally
nerviosamente nervously
no no; not
nombre: en nombre de on behalf of
normalmente normally; usually
novedad: sin novedad safely
nunca never; ever
paciencia: con paciencia patiently
para for; to
  para atrás backwards; **para la
  derecha** towards the right; **para
  siempre** forever
parte: de mi parte on my behalf
  en cualquier parte anywhere; **en
  gran parte** largely

en otra parte elsewhere
  en parte partly, in part; **en todas
  partes** everywhere; **por otra
  parte** on the other hand
peligrosamente dangerously
peor worse
  el peor the worst
perfectamente perfectly
persona: por persona per person
personalmente personally
pesadamente heavily
pesar: a pesar de despite; in spite of
  a pesar de que even though
pie: a pie on foot
poco not very; not a lot; not much
  poco a poco little by little, bit by bit
por because of; for; by; through
  por qué why
precisamente precisely, exactly
primero first
principalmente mainly
principio: al principio at first
probable likely
probablemente probably
profundamente deeply
pronto soon
propósito: a propósito
  deliberately; on purpose
qué how
querer: sin querer accidentally
quién: de quién/de quiénes whose
rápidamente fast, quickly
rápido quickly
realidad: en realidad in fact, actually
realmente really
recientemente recently, lately
regularmente regularly, on a
  regular basis
relativamente relatively

repente: **de repente** suddenly
seguida: **en seguida** right away
seguido straight on
   todo seguido straight on
según according to; depending on
seguramente probably; surely
sencillamente simply
sentido: **en este sentido** in this
   respect
separado: **por separado** separately
ser: **a no ser que** unless
serio: **en serio** seriously
sí yes
siempre always
   como siempre as usual
siguiente: **al/el día siguiente** next
   day
silencio: **en silencio** quietly; in
   silence
silenciosamente quietly, silently
sin without **sin embargo** still,
   however, nonetheless
siquiera: **ni siquiera** not even
sitio: **en algún sitio** somewhere
   en ningún sitio nowhere
sobre on; over; about
solamente only; solely
sólo only; solely
   tan sólo only, just
suavemente gently; softly; smoothly
suelo: **al suelo** to the ground
   en el suelo on the ground
sumamente highly, extremely
supuesto: **por supuesto** of course
tal: **tal como** just as
   tal y como están las cosas under
   the circumstances; **tal vez**
   perhaps, maybe
también also, too

tampoco not...either, neither
tan so; such
   tan ... como as ... as
tanto so much; so often
   tanto más all the more
tarde late
   más tarde later; afterwards
temprano early
   más temprano earlier
tiempo: **a tiempo** in time; on time
   al mismo tiempo at the same
   time; **mucho tiempo** long
todavía still; yet; even
todo: **en todo/toda** throughout
   todo lo más at (the) most
total in short; at the end of the day
   en total altogether, in all
totalmente totally, completely
través: **a través de** through; across
vano: **en vano** in vain
velocidad: **a toda velocidad** at full
   speed, at top speed
ver: **por lo visto** apparently
vez: **algunas veces** sometimes
   cada vez más more and more;
   cada vez menos less and less; **de
   vez en cuando** from time to time,
   now and then; **en vez de** instead
   of; **rara vez** rarely, seldom; **una
   vez** once; **una vez más** once more
vía: **en vías de** on its way to
   en vías de desarrollo developing;
   en vías de extinción endangered
vista: **de vista** by sight
   en vista de in view of
voz: **en voz alta** aloud; loudly
   en voz baja in a low voice
ya already
   ya mismo at once; **ya no** not any
   more, no longer

SOME EXTRA NOUNS

What is a noun?
A **noun** is a 'naming' word for a living being, thing or idea, for *example*, *woman*, *desk*, *happiness*, *Andrew*.

la **abertura** opening
el **abismo** gulf
el **aburrimiento** boredom
el **abuso** abuse
el **acceso** access
la **acción** (*pl* acciones) action
el **acento** accent
el **ácido** acid
el **acontecimiento** event
la **actitud** attitude
la **actividad** activity
el **acuerdo** agreement; settlement
la **advertencia** warning
la **afirmación** (*pl* afirmaciones) claim
la **agencia** agency
la **agenda** diary
el/la **agente** agent
la **agitación** (*pl* agitaciones) stir
el **agujero** hole
la **alcantarilla** drain
la **alcayata** hook
la **alegría** joy
el **alfabeto** alphabet
el **alfiler** pin
el/la **aliado/a** ally
el **aliento** breath
el **alivio** relief
el **alma** (*f*) soul
el **almacén** (*pl* almacenes) store
el/la **amante** lover
la **ambición** (*pl* ambiciones) ambition
la **amenaza** threat
el/la **amigo(a)** mate

la **amistad** friendship
el **amor** love
el **análisis** (*pl inv*) analysis
la **anchura** breadth; width
el/la **anfitrión(ona)** host
el **ángel** angel
el **ángulo** angle
la **angustia** anguish
el **animal doméstico** pet
la **antigüedad** antique
el **anuncio** announcement
el **anzuelo** hook
el **apoyo** support
la **aprobación** (*pl* aprobaciones) approval
la **apuesta** bet; stake
la **armada** navy
el **arreglo** compromise
la **artesanía** craft
el **artículo** article; item
la **asociación** (*pl* asociaciones) association
el **asombro** astonishment
el **aspecto** aspect
la **astilla** splinter
el **asunto** affair
el **atajo** short-cut
el **ataúd** coffin
la **atención** (*pl* atenciones) attention
el **atentado** attempt
la **atracción; el atractivo** attraction
la **ausencia** absence
la **autoridad** authority

la **aventura** adventure; affair
el **aviso** notice
la **ayuda** assistance, help
el/la **ayudante** assistant
el **ayuntamiento** council
el **azar** chance
la **bala** bullet
la **bañera** tub
la **barandilla** rail
la **barrera** barrier
el **barril** barrel
la **base** base
la **batalla** battle
la **batería** battery
la **beca** grant
el **beso** kiss
la **Biblia** Bible
la **bolsa** bag
la **bomba** bomb
la **bondad** kindness
el **borde** edge
la **broma** joke
el **brote** outbreak
el **bullicio** bustle
la **burbuja** bubble
el **cable** cable
la **caja** box
la **calcomanía** transfer
el **cálculo** calculation
el **caldo** stock
la **calidad** quality
la **calma** calm
el **camino** path; way
el **campamento** camp
la **campaña** campaign
el **camping** (*pl* ~s) site
el **canal** channel
el/la **canguro** baby-sitter
la **cantidad** amount

el **caos** chaos
la **capa** layer
la **capacidad** ability; capacity
el **capítulo** chapter
la **característica** characteristic;
   feature
la **caridad** charity
el/la **catedrático(a)** professor
el **cazo** pot
los **celos** jealousy (*sing*)
el **centro** centre; focus; middle
el **centro turístico** resort
la **cesta** basket
el **chiste** joke
el **cielo** heaven
el **cierre** closure
la **cima** top
el **círculo** circle
las **circunstancias** circumstances
la **cita** quote; extract; appointment
el/la **civil** civilian
la **civilización** (*pl* civilizaciones)
   civilization
la **clase** sort; period
la **clasificación** (*pl* clasificaciones)
   classification
la **clave** code
la **codicia** greed
la **columna** column
el **columpio** swing
la **combinación** (*pl* combinaciones)
   combination
el **combustible** fuel
el **comentario** comment, remark
el/la **comentarista** commentator
las **comillas: entre comillas**
   inverted commas: in quotes
la **comisión** (*pl* comisiones)
   commission

el comité (*pl* comités) committee
el compañero fellow
la comparación (*pl* comparaciones) comparison
la compasión (*pl* compasiones) sympathy
la competición (*pl* competiciones) contest
el/la competidor(a) rival
la comprensión (*pl* comprensiones) sympathy
el compromiso commitment
la comunicación (*pl* comunicaciones) communication
la comunidad community
la concentración (*pl* concentraciones) concentration
la conciencia conscience
la condecoración (*pl* condecoraciones) honour
la condición (*pl* condiciones) condition; status
la conducta conduct
la conexión (*pl* conexiones) connection
la conferencia conference
la confianza confidence
el conflicto conflict
el confort comfort
el congreso conference
la conmoción (*pl* conmociones) shock; disturbance
el conocimiento consciousness; knowledge
la consecuencia consequence
el consejo advice
la construcción (*pl* construcciones) construction; structure
el/la consumidor(a) consumer

el contacto contact
el contenido content
el contexto context
el contorno outline
el contraste contrast
la contribución (*pl* contribución) contribution
la conversación (*pl* conversaciones) conversation
la copia copy
el corazón (*pl* corazones) heart; core
la corona crown
el/la corresponsal correspondent
la corrupción (*pl* corrupciones) corruption
la cortesía politeness
la cosa thing
las cosas stuff (*sing*)
la costumbre custom
el crecimiento growth
el/la criado(a) servant
la crisis (*pl inv*) crisis
la crítica criticism
el cuadro picture
la cuba tub
el cubierto place
el cuchicheo whispering
la cuenta count
   por su cuenta of his own accord
el cuento tale
la cuestión (*pl* cuestiones) question
la cueva cave
el cuidado care
la culpa blame
la cultura culture
la cuota fee
la curiosidad curiosity
los datos data (*pl*)
el debate debate

el deber duty
la decepción (*pl* decepciones) disappointment
la decisión (*pl* decisiones) decision
el defecto fault
la definición (*pl* definiciones) definition
el/la dependiente(a) assistant
la depresión (*pl* depresiones) depression
el/la derecho(a) right
los derechos fee
el desagüe drain
el desarrollo development
el desastre disaster
el descanso break
el/la desconocido(a) stranger
la desdicha unhappiness
el deseo desire; wish; urge
el desgarrón (*pl* desgarrones) tear
la desgracia misfortune
el desorden disorder; mess
el destino destiny; fate
la destreza skill
la destrucción (*pl* destrucciones) destruction
la desventaja disadvantage
el detalle detail
la devolución (*pl* devoluciones) refund; return
el diagrama diagram
el diálogo dialogue
la diana target
el diario diary; journal
la diferencia difference
la dificultad difficulty
la dimensión (*pl* dimensiones) dimension
el Dios God

el/la diplomático(a) diplomat
el/la diputado(a) deputy
la dirección (*pl* direcciones) direction
la disciplina discipline
el discurso speech
la discusión (*pl* discusiones) argument; discussion
el diseño design
el dispositivo device
la disputa dispute
la distancia distance
la división (*pl* divisiones) division
el drama drama
la duda doubt
el eco echo
la economía economics (*sing*); economy
la edición (*pl* ediciones) edition
el efecto effect
el ejemplar copy
el ejemplo example
por ejemplo for instance
el/la elector(a) elector
la elegancia elegance
el elemento element
la encuesta survey
el/la enemigo(a) enemy
la energía energy
el entusiasmo enthusiasm; excitement
la envidia envy
la época period
el equilibrio balance
el equipo equipment
el error mistake
el escándalo scandal
el escape leak
la escasez shortage
la escritura writing

el **esfuerzo** effort
el **espacio** space
la **espalda** back
la **especie** species (*sing*)
el **espectáculo** show; sight
la **esperanza** hope
el **espesor**; la **espesura** thickness
el **esquema** outline; diagram
la **estaca** stake
la **estancia** stay
la **estatua** statue
el **estilo** style
la **estrategia** strategy
el **estrés** stress
la **estructura** structure
el **estudio** studio
la **estupidez** (*pl* estupideces)
   stupidity
la **etapa** stage
la **excepción** (*pl* excepciones)
   exception
el **exceso** excess
la **excusa** excuse
el/la **exiliado(a)** exile
el **exilio** exile
las **existencias** stock
el **éxito** success
la **experiencia** experience
el/la **experto(a)** expert
la **explicación** (*pl* explicaciones)
   explanation
la **explosión** (*pl* explosiones)
   explosion
   una **explosión** a bomb blast
las **exportaciones** exports
la **exposición** (*pl* exposiciones)
   exhibition
la **expresión** (*pl* expresiones)
   expression

la **extensión** (*pl* extensiones) extent
el **extracto** extract
el/la **extranjero(a)** foreigner
la **fabricación** (*pl* fabricaciones)
   manufacture
la **facilidad** facility
el **factor** factor
el **fallo** failure
la **falta**: absence
   falta (de) lack (of)
la **fama** reputation
el **favor** favour
la **fe** faith
la **felicidad** happiness
la **fila** row
la **filosofía** philosophy
el **fin** end
la **flecha** arrow
el **fondo** background; bottom; fund
el/la **forastero(a)** stranger
la **forma** form; shape
la **fortuna** fortune
el **fracaso** failure
la **frase** sentence; phrase
la **frente** front
el **frescor**, la **frescura** freshness
la **fuente** source
la **fuerza** force; strength
la **función** (*pl* funciones) function
la **ganancia** gain
el **gancho** hook
los **gastos** expenses
la **generación** (*pl* generaciones)
   generation
el **gol** goal
el **golfo** gulf
el **golpe** bang; blow; knock
la **gotera** leak
el **grado** degree

el gráfico chart
la grieta crack
el grito cry
el grupo group
la guía guide
el hambre (f) hunger
el hecho fact
la higiene hygiene
la hilera row
el honor honour
los honorarios fee
la honra honour
el hueco gap
la huella trace
el humo fumes (pl); smoke
el humor humour
la idea idea
   no tengo ni idea I haven't a clue
el idioma language
el/la idiota fool; idiot
la imagen (pl imágenes) image
la imaginación (pl imaginaciones) imagination
el impacto impact
el imperio empire
las importaciones imports
la importancia importance
la impresión (pl impresiones) impression
el impuesto duty
el impulso urge
la inauguración (pl inauguraciones) opening
el incidente incident
la independencia independence
el índice index
la indirecta hint
la infancia childhood
el infierno hell

la influencia influence
los ingresos earnings
el/la inspector(a) inspector
el instante instant
el intervalo gap
la institución (pl instituciones) institution
el instituto institute
las instrucciones instructions
el instrumento instrument
la intención (pl intenciones) intention; aim
el interés (pl intereses) interest
la interrupción (pl interrupciones) interruption
la investigación (pl investigaciones) research
la invitación (pl invitaciones) invitation
la ira anger
el jaleo row
el/la jefe(a) chief
el juego gambling
el juguete toy
la lágrima tear
la lata can
el/la lector(a) reader
la leyenda legend; caption
la libertad freedom
la licenciatura degree
el/la líder leader
la liga league
el límite boundary; limit
la limpieza cleanliness
la línea line
la liquidación (pl liquidaciones) settlement
la lista list
la literatura literature

el local premises (*pl*)
la locura madness
el logro achievement
la loncha slice
la longitud length
el lugar site
el lujo luxury
la luz (*pl* luces) light
  luz de la luna moonlight
el/la maestro(a) master
la magia magic
la manera manner
la máquina machine
la marca brand; mark
el marco frame
el margen (*pl* márgenes) margin
la máscara mask
la matrícula fee
el máximo maximum
la mayoría majority
el medio (de) means (of)
la mejora, la mejoría improvement
la memoria memory
la mente mind
el método method
la mezcla mixture
el miedo fear
el milagro miracle
la mina mine
el mínimo minimum
el ministerio ministry
la minoría minority
la mirada glance
la misa mass
la misión (*pl* misiones) mission
el misterio mystery
el mitin (*pl* mítines) rally
el mito myth
la moda fashion; trend

la molestia annoyance
el molino mill
el montón (*pl* montones) mass; pile
la moral morals (*pl*)
el mordisco bite
el motivo pattern
el motor motor
el muchacho lad
la muchedumbre crowd
la muestra sample
la muñeca doll
la naturaleza nature
el naufragio wreckage (*sing*)
la negociación (*pl* negociaciones)
  negotiation
el nervio nerve
la niñez childhood
el nivel level
el nombramiento appointment
la nota note
el número number; issue
la objeción (*pl* objeciones) objection
el objetivo objective; purpose;
  target
el objeto object; goal
las obras works
el odio hate
el/la oficial officer
la olla pot
el olor smell
la opción (*pl* opciones) option
la opinión (*pl* opiniones) opinion
la oportunidad chance; opportunity
la oposición (*pl* oposiciones)
  opposition
la orden (*pl* órdenes) order
la organización (*pl* organizaciones)
  organization
  organización benéfica charity

el orgullo pride
el origen (*pl* orígenes) origin
la oscuridad darkness
la paciencia patience
la página page
la paja straw
la palabra word
el palacio palace
el palo stick
el pánico panic
el paquete pack; packet
la pareja pair
la parte part
  parte de arriba top; **parte
  delantera** front; **parte trasera** rear;
  de parte de algn on behalf of sb
la partida item
el parto labour
  estar de parto to be in labour
el pasaje; el pasillo passage
la pasión (*pl* pasiones) passion
el paso footstep
el patrón (*pl* patrones) pattern
la pausa pause
el payaso clown
el pedazo piece
el pedido order
la pelea row
el peligro danger
la pena distress; penalty
el penalty (*pl* penalties) penalty
el pensamiento thought
el periódico journal
el periodo period
el/la perito(a) expert
el permiso permission
la persona person
el personal personnel
la perspectiva prospect

la pesadilla nightmare
la picadura bite
la pieza piece; item
la pila battery; pile
la pista clue
el placer delight; pleasure
el plan plan; scheme
el plato dish
la plaza place
el poder power
el poema poem
la política politics (*sing*); policy
la póliza policy
el polvo dust
la pompa bubble
el porcentaje percentage
la porción (*pl* porciones) portion
el portavoz (*pl* portavoces)
  spokesman
la posibilidad possibility
la posición (*pl* posiciones) position
la práctica practice
la preferencia choice
el prefijo code
la pregunta question
el premio award
la preparación (*pl* preparaciones)
  preparation
los preparativos arrangements
la presencia presence
la presión (*pl* presiones) pressure
el presupuesto budget; quote
la princesa princess
el príncipe prince
el principio beginning; principle
la prioridad priority
el problema problem; trouble
el proceso process
el/la profesor(a) master

la **profundidad** depth
el **programa** schedule
la **prohibición** (*pl* prohibiciones) ban
el **propósito** purpose
  a **propósito** on purpose
la **propuesta** proposal
la **prosperidad** prosperity
la **protección** (*pl* protecciones)
  protection
la **protesta** protest
las **provisiones** provisions
el **proyecto** plan
la **publicidad** publicity
la **puja** bid
la **punta** point
la **puntería** aim
el **punto** item; point
  punto de partida starting point;
  punto de vista point of view
el/la **querido(a)** darling
la **rabia** rage
la **raja** crack
el **rato** while
la **razón** (*pl* razones) reason
la **reacción** (*pl* reacciones) reaction;
  response
la **realidad** reality
la **rebanada** slice
el/la **rebelde** rebel
el **recado** message
la **recepción** (*pl* recepciones)
  reception
la **recesión** (*pl* recesiones) recession
la **reclamación** (*pl* reclamaciones)
  claim
el **recuerdo** souvenir
el **recurso** resource
  como último recurso as a last resort
la **red** network

la **reducción** (*pl* reducciones)
  reduction
la **reforma** reform
la **regla** period
la **reina** queen
la **relación** (*pl* relaciones) relationship
la **religión** (*pl* religiones) religion
la **reputación** (*pl* reputaciones) status
el **requisito** requirement
la **reserva** fund; stock
la **resistencia** resistance
la **resolución** (*pl* resoluciones)
  resolution
el **respecto: con respecto a** with
  regard to
el **respeto** respect
la **respiración** (*pl* respiraciones) breath
la **responsabilidad** responsibility
la **respuesta** reply; response
los **restos** remains; wreckage (*sing*)
el **resultado** outcome
el **reto** challenge
el **retrato** portrait
la **reunión** (*pl* reuniones) meeting
la **revista** magazine; journal
el **rey** (*pl* ~es) king
el **riel** rail
el **ritmo** pace
el/la **rival** rival
la **rodaja** slice
el **ruido** noise
la **ruina** ruin
el **rumor** rumour
la **ruptura** break
la **rutina** routine
el **sacrificio** sacrifice
el/la **santo(a)** saint
la **sección** (*pl* secciones) section
el **secreto** secret

el **sector** sector
la **sed** thirst
la **tidad** security; safety
la **selección** (*pl* selecciones)
  selection; choice
el **sentido** sense; way
el **sentimiento** feeling
la **señal** sign; mark
el **señor** lord
el **servicio** service
la **sesión** (*pl* sesiones) session
el **significado** meaning
el **silbato** whistle
el **silencio** silence
el **símbolo** symbol
el **sindicato** trade union
el **sistema** system
el **sitio** place
la **situación** (*pl* situaciones) situation
el/la **socio(a)** member
la **soledad** loneliness
el **sollozo** sob
la **solución** (*pl* soluciones) solution
la **sombra** shadow
el **sondeo (de opinión)** poll
el **sonido** sound
la **sorpresa** surprise
la **sospecha** suspicion
la **subasta** auction
el **subtítulo** caption
la **subvención** (*pl* subvenciones)
  grant
la **suciedad** dirtiness
el **sueño** sleep
la **suerte** luck
  buena/mala suerte good/bad luck
la **sugerencia** suggestion
el **suicidio** suicide
la **suma** sum

la **superficie** surface
la **supervisión** (*pl* supervisiones)
  supervision
el/la **superviviente** survivor
el/la **suplente** substitute
el **surtido** choice
la **sustancia** substance
el/la **sustituto(a)** substitute
la **táctica** tactics (*pl*)
el **talento** talent
la **tapa** top
la **tapicería, el tapiz** (*pl* tapices)
  tapestry
el **tapón** (*pl* tapones) top
la **tarea** task
la **tarifa; la tasa** rate
el **teatro** theatre; drama
la **técnica** technique
la **tecnología** technology
el **tema** theme; issue
la **tendencia** trend
la **tensión** (*pl* tensiones) tension;
  strain
la **tentativa** attempt; bid
la **teoría** theory
el **territorio** territory
el **terrón** (*pl* terrones) lump
el **texto** text
la **tienda** store
la **timidez** shyness
el **tipo** type; kind; fellow, guy
el **tío** (*Sp*) guy
la **tirada** edition
el **título** title
el **tomo** volume
la **tortura** torture
el **total** total
la **tradición** (*pl* tradiciones)
  tradition

la **trampa** trap
la **tranquilidad** calmness
la **transferencia** transfer
el **tratamiento** treatment
el **trato** deal; treatment
la **tristeza** sadness
el **trozo** bit; piece; slice
el **truco** trick
el **tubo** tube
la **tumba** grave
el **tumor** growth
el **turno** turn
la **unidad** unit
la **valentía** bravery, courage
el **valor** value
el **vapor** steam
la **variedad** variety; range
la **vela** candle
el **veneno** poison

la **ventaja** advantage; asset
la **verdad** truth
la **vergüenza** shame
la **versión** (*pl* versiones) version
la **victoria** victory
la **vida** life
el **vínculo** bond
la **violencia** violence
la **visita**; visit; visitor
el/la **visitante** visitor
la **vista** sight
el **volumen** (*pl* volúmenes) volume
el/la **voluntario(a)** volunteer
el/la **votante** voter
la **vuelta** turn; return
   dar una **vuelta** to go for a stroll;
   dar una **vuelta en bicicleta** to go
   for a bike ride

VERBS

> **What is a verb?**
> A **verb** is a 'doing' word which describes what someone or something does, what someone or something is, or what happens to them, for example, *be*, *sing*, *live*.

abandonar to abandon
abrigar(se) to shelter
abrir to turn on
  abrir(se) to open
abrochar to fasten
aburrir to bore
  aburrirse to get bored
acabar de hacer algo to have just done sth
acampar to camp
aceptar to accept
acercarse (a) to approach
  acercarse a to go towards
aclarar(se) to clear
acompañar to accompany; to go with
aconsejar to advise; to suggest
acordarse de to remember
acostarse to lie down
acostumbrarse a algo/algn to get used to sth/sb
actuar to act; to operate
acusar to accuse
adaptar to adapt
adelantar to go forward; to overtake
adivinar to guess
admirar to admire
admitir to admit
adoptar to adopt
adorar to adore
adquirir to acquire; to purchase
afectar to affect
afirmar to assert; to state

agarrar to catch; to grab; to grasp
agradecer to thank (for)
aguantar to bear
ahorrar to save
ahuyentar to chase (off)
alcanzar to reach
  alcanzar a algn to catch up with sb;
  alcanzar a ver to catch sight of
alimentar to nourish
aliviar to relieve
almacenar to store
alojarse to put up
  alojarse con to lodge with
alquilar to hire; to rent: to let
amar to love
amenazar to threaten
amontonar to stack
andar to walk
anhelar to long for
animar to encourage
  animar a algn a hacer algo to
  urge sb to do sth
anunciar to advertise; to announce
añadir to add
apagar to switch off; to turn off; to put out
apagar to turn off
  apagarse to fade
aparecer to appear
apetecer to fancy
  me apetece un helado I fancy an ice cream

aplastar to crush
aplaudir to applaud; to cheer; to clap
aplazar to postpone; to put back
aplicar a to apply to
apostar (a) to bet (on)
apoyar to support; to endorse
  apoyar(se) to lean
apreciar to appreciate
aprender to learn
apretar to press; to squeeze
aprobar to approve of; to endorse
aprovechar to take advantage (of)
apuntar to take down
arañar to scratch
arrancar to pull out
arrastrar to drag
  arrastrarse to crawl
arreglar to fix (up); to arrange; to settle
  arreglárselas to cope; to manage
arrepentirse de to regret
arriesgar to risk
arrojar to hurl
arruinar to ruin
asar to bake
ascender to promote
asegurar to assure; to ensure;
  to secure
asentir con la cabeza to nod
asfixiar(se) to suffocate
asistir (a) to attend
asombrar to amaze; to astonish
asustar to alarm; to frighten; to
  startle
atacar to attack
atar to attach; to tie
atender to treat
  atender a to attend to
atraer to attract
atrasar to hold up

atreverse (a hacer algo) to dare
  (to do sth)
aumentar to increase; to raise
avanzar to advance
averiarse to break down
averiguar to check
avisar to warn
ayudar to help
azotar to whip
bailar to dance
bajar: to come down; to go down;
  to lower
  bajar (de): to get off; bajar de to
  get out of
balbucir to stammer
barrer to sweep
basar algo en to base sth on
batir to whip; to beat
besar to kiss
bombardear to bomb
brillar to shine; to sparkle
bromear to joke
burlarse de to make fun of
buscar to look for; to search; to seek
caerse to fall (down)
  se me cayó I dropped it
calcular to estimate
calentar(se) to heat (up)
callarse to be quiet
cambiar to alter; to exchange
  cambiar(se) to change
cancelar to cancel
cantar to sing
capturar to capture
carecer de to lack
cargar (de) to load (with)
causar to cause
cavar to dig
celebrar to celebrate

centellear to sparkle
cerrar: to turn off: to close; to fasten
  cerrar(se): to shut; cerrar con
  llave to lock
charlar to chat
chillar to scream
chismear to gossip
chocar con to bump into
chupar to suck
citar to quote
clasificarse to qualify
cobrar to claim; to get
coger to catch; to grab; to seize
colaborar to collaborate
coleccionar to collect
colgar to hang (up)
colocar to place
combinar to combine
comenzar (a) to start (to)
cometer to commit
compaginar to combine
comparar to compare
compartir to share
compensar to compensate (for)
  compensar por to make up for
competir en to compete in
complacer to please
completar to complete; to make up
comprar (a) to buy (from)
comprender to comprise
comunicar to communicate
conceder to grant
concentrarse to concentrate
concertar to arrange
concluir to conclude; to accomplish
condenar to condemn; to sentence
conducir to lead
conectar to connect
confesar to confess

confiar to trust
  confiar en to rely on
confirmar to confirm
confundir (con) to confuse (with)
  confundir a algn con to mistake
  sb for
congelar to freeze
conocer to know
conseguir to achieve; to get; to secure
  conseguir (hacer) to succeed (in
  doing)
considerar to consider; to rate
constar de to consist of
  hacer constar to record
constituir to constitute; to make up
construir to build; to put up
consultar to consult
consumir to consume
contar to count
  contar con to depend on
contemplar to contemplate
contener to contain; to hold
contestar to answer
continuar to continue; to keep;
  to resume
contribuir to contribute
controlar to control
convencer to convince
convenir to suit
convertir to convert
copiar to copy
correr to run
cortar to cut (off); to mow
costar to cost
crear to create
crecer to grow
creer to believe; to reckon
criar to bring up
criticar to criticize

cruzar to cross
cubrir (de) to cover (with)
cuchichear to whisper
cuidar to look after; to take care of; to mind
  cuidar de to take care of
cultivar to cultivate
cumplir to accomplish; to carry out
curar to heal
dañar to harm
dar to give:
  dar a to overlook; dar asco a to disgust; dar de comer a to feed; dar la bienvenida to welcome; dar marcha atrás to reverse; dar saltitos to hop; dar un paseo to go for a stroll; dar un puñetazo a to punch; dar una bofetada a to slap; dar vergüenza a to embarrass; dar vuelta a to turn; darse cuenta de algo to become aware of sth; darse por vencido to give up; darse prisa to hurry;
deber must; to owe
  deber hacer algo to be supposed to do sth; debo hacerlo I must do it
decepcionar to disappoint
decidir(se) (a) to decide (to)
decidirse (a) to make up one's mind (to)
decir to say; to tell
declarar to declare
  declarar culpable to convict; declararse en huelga to (go on) strike
decorar to decorate
dedicar to devote
defender to defend
definir to define

dejar to leave
  dejar caer to drop
deletrear to spell
demorar(se) to delay
demostrar to demonstrate
depender de to depend on
derribar to demolish
desanimar to discourage
desaparecer to disappear
desarrollar(se) to develop
descansar to rest
descargar to unload
describir to describe
descubrir to discover; to find out
desear to desire; to wish
deshacerse de to get rid of
deslizar(se) to slip
desnudarse to strip
despedir to dismiss
despegar to take off
despejar(se) to clear
despertar(se) to wake up
desprenderse to come off
desteñirse to fade
destruir to smash
desviar to divert
detener to arrest
determinar to determine
detestar to detest
devolver to bring back; to give back; to send back
  devolver a su sitio to put back
dibujar to draw
diferenciarse (de) to differ (from)
dimitir to resign
dirigir to conduct; to direct; to manage
disculparse (de) to apologise (for)
discutir to argue; to debate; to discuss

diseñar to design

disfrazar to disguise

disfrutar to enjoy

disminuir to decline; to decrease; to diminish

distinguir to distinguish

distribuir to distribute

divertir to divert
  divertirse to enjoy oneself

dividir to divide; to split

doblar to fold
  doblar(se) to double

dominar to dominate; to master

ducharse to shower

dudar to doubt

durar to last

echar to pour:
  echar a algn to throw sb out;
  echar a algn la culpa de algo
  to blame sb for sth; **echar al correo**
  to post; **echar de menos** to miss;
  echar una mirada a algo to glance
  at sth; **echarse** to lie; **echarse a**
  llorar to burst into tears; **echarse**
  a reír to burst out laughing

educar to bring up; to educate

ejecutar to execute

elegir to choose; to select; to elect

elogiar to praise

emocionar to excite

empatar to draw, to tie

empezar (a) to begin (to)

emplear to employ

empujar to push

encarcelar to imprison

encender to switch on; to turn on; to light

encerrar to shut in

encontrar to find; to meet

enfocar to focus

enjugar to wipe

enseñar to teach; to show

entender to understand

enterarse de to hear about

enterrar to bury

entrar (en) to enter

entregarse to give oneself up; to surrender

entrevistar to interview

enviar to send

envolver to wrap up

equivocarse to make a mistake; to be mistaken

erigir to erect

escapar (de) to escape (from)

escarbar to dig

escoger to choose; to pick

esconderse to hide

escuchar to listen (to)

especializarse en to specialize in

especular to gamble

esperar to wait (for); to expect; to hope

establecer to establish; to set up
  establecerse to settle

estallar to blow up

estar to be
  estar acostumbrado a algo/
  algn to be used to sth/sb; **estar de**
  acuerdo to agree; **estar de pie** to
  be standing; **estar dispuesto a**
  hacer algo to be prepared to do
  sth; to be willing to do sth;
  estar equivocado to be wrong;
  estar involucrado en algo to be
  involved in sth

estirar(se) to stretch (out)

estrecharse la mano to shake hands

estrellar(se) to crash
estropear to ruin
  estropear(se) to spoil
estudiar to study; to investigate
evitar (hacer) to avoid (doing)
exagerar to exaggerate
examinar to examine
  examinarse to sit an exam
excitar to excite
exclamar to exclaim
excluir to exclude; to suspend
existir to exist
experimentar to experience
explicar to explain
explorar to explore
explotar to explode
exponer to display
exportar to export
expresar to express
exprimir to squeeze
expulsar temporalmente to suspend
extender to spread: to extend
  extender(se) to spread out
extrañar (*LAm*) to miss
fabricar to manufacture
faltar to be lacking; to fail
felicitar to congratulate
fiarse de to trust
financiar to finance
fingir to pretend (to)
firmar to sign
flotar to float
fluir to flow
formar(se) to form
forzar a algn a hacer (algo) to force
  sb to do (sth)
fotografiar to photograph
frecuentar to frequent
freír to fry

funcionar to work
  (hacer) funcionar to operate
fustigar to whip
ganar to earn; to gain
garantizar to guarantee
gastar to spend: to waste
  gastar(se) to wear (out)
gemir to groan
golpear to knock; to beat
grabar to record
gritar to shout; to scream; to cry
guardar to keep; to store
guiar to guide
gustar to like
haber to have
hablar to speak; to talk
hacer to do; to make; to bake
  hacer añicos to shatter; **hacer
  campaña** to campaign; **hacer
  comentarios** to comment; **hacer
  daño a** to hurt; **hacer las maletas**
  to pack; **hacer preguntas** to ask
  questions; **hacer público** to issue;
  hacer señas *or* **una señal** to
  signal; **hacer una lista de** to list;
  hacer una oferta to bid; **hacer
  una pausa** to pause; **hacer una
  señal con la mano** to wave;
  hacerse to become; to get;
  hacerse adulto to grow up;
  hacer(se) pedazos to smash
helarse to freeze
herir to injure
hervir to boil
huir to flee; to run away *or* off
identificar to identify
iluminar(se) to light
imaginar to imagine
impedir to prevent (from)

implicar to imply; to involve
imponer to impose
importar to matter; to mind; to care
  ¡no me importa! I don't care!;
  ¿y a quién le importa? who cares?
impresionar to impress
imprimir to print
inclinar to bend
  inclinarse to bend down
incluir to include
indicar to point out; to indicate
influir to influence
informar to inform
inscribirse to register
insinuar to hint
insinuar to imply
insistir en to insist on
instruir to educate
insultar to insult
intentar to attempt to
interesar to interest
  interesarse por to be interested in
interrogar to question
interrumpir to interrupt
introducir to introduce
invadir to invade
investigar to investigate
invitar to invite
  invitar a algn a algo to treat sb to sth
ir to go
  ir a buscar a algn to fetch sb;
  ir bien a to suit; **ir deprisa** to dash;
  ir en bicicleta to ride a bike
irse to go away
irritar to irritate; to aggravate
jugar to play; to gamble
juntarse con to join
jurar to swear
justificar to justify

juzgar to judge
lamentarse to moan
lamer to lick
lanzar to throw; to launch
  lanzarse a to rush into
leer to read
levantar to raise; to put up; to lift
  levantarse to get up; to rise
limpiar to clean
llamar to call
  llamar por teléfono: to ring;
  llamarse to be called
llegar to arrive
llenar (de) to fill (with)
llevar: to carry; to bear; to wear
  llevar a cabo to carry out;
  llevarse to take
llorar to cry, weep
llover to rain
  llover a cántaros to pour
luchar to fight; to struggle
maltratar to abuse
manchar to dirty
mandar to command, to order
manifestarse to demonstrate
mantener to maintain; to support
  mantener el equilibrio to balance
marcharse to depart; to leave
medir to measure
mejorar(se) to improve
mencionar to mention
mentir to lie
merecer to deserve
meterse en to get into
mezclar to mix
mimar to spoil
mirar to look (at); to watch
  mirar fijamente to stare at
modificar to adjust

molestar to annoy; to disturb; to trouble
montar a caballo to ride
morder to bite
morir to die
mostrar to hold up
  mostrar(se) to show
mover to move
multiplicar to multiply
nacer to be born
necesitar to need
negar to deny
  negarse (a) to refuse (to)
negociar to negotiate
notar to note
obedecer to obey
obligar a algn a to oblige sb to
observar to notice; to observe
obstruir to block
obtener to obtain
ocasionar to bring about
ocultar to hide
ocupar to occupy
  ocuparse de to deal with
ocurrir to occur
odiar to hate
ofender to offend
ofrecer to offer
  ofrecerse a hacer algo to volunteer to do sth
oír to hear
oler to smell
olvidar to forget
operar a algn to operate on sb
oponerse a to oppose; to object to
organizar(se) to organize
otorgar to award
pagar to pay
pararse to come to a halt, to stop

parecer to seem (to); to look
  parecerse a to look like, to resemble
participar en to take part in
partir to share
  partir(se) to split
pasar to pass; to overtake; to spend
pedir to request; to order
  pedir a algn que haga algo to ask sb to do sth; **pedir algo a algn** to ask sb for sth; **pedir algo prestado a algn** to borrow sth from sb
pegar to hit; to stick; to strike
pensar to think
  pensar en to think about; **pensar hacer** to intend to do
perder to miss:
  perder a algn de vista to lose sight of sb
perdonar a to forgive
perdurar to survive
permitir to allow, to permit, to let
  permitirse to afford
perseguir to pursue
persuadir to persuade
pertenecer a to belong to
pesar to weigh
picar to bite
pinchar(se) to burst
planchar to iron
plegar to fold
poder to be able to; can; might
  ¿puedo llamar por teléfono?: can I use your phone?; **el profesor podría venir ahora:** the teacher might come now; **puede que venga más tarde** he might come later
poner to put; to lay
  poner de relieve to highlight; **poner en duda** to question; **poner**

en el suelo to put down; poner en orden to tidy; ponerse to put on; ponerse de pie to stand up; ponerse en contacto con to contact

portarse to behave

poseer to own, to possess

practicar to practise

precipitarse to rush

predecir to predict

preferir to prefer

preguntar (por) to inquire (about)
  preguntarse to wonder

prender fuego to catch fire

preocupar to trouble; to bother
  preocuparse (por) to worry (about)

preparar(se) to prepare

prescindir de to do without

presentar to present; to introduce

prestar to lend

prevenir to warn

prever to foresee

privar to deprive

probar to prove

producir to produce

prohibir to ban; to forbid

prometer to promise

pronosticar to predict

pronunciar to pronounce

propagarse to spread

proponer to propose

proteger to protect

protestar to protest

proveer to provide

publicar to publish

quedar to remain
  quedarse to stay

quejarse (de) to complain (about)

quemar to burn

querer to want (to); to love; to like

quitar to remove
  quitar algo a algn to take sth from sb; quitarse to take off

reaccionar to react; to respond

realizar to fulfil; to realize

reanudar to resume

recalcar to emphasize; to stress

rechazar to reject

recibir to receive
  recibirse (LAm) to qualify

reclamar to demand; to claim

recoger to pick (up); to collect; to gather

recomendar to recommend

reconocer to recognize

recordar to recall
  recordarle a algn to remind sb of

recuperarse to recover

reducir(se) to reduce

reembolsar to refund

referirse a to refer (to)
  en lo que se refiere a ... as regards ...

reflejar, reflexionar to reflect

reformar to reform

regañar to tell off

regar to water

registrar to register; to examine

reír to laugh
  reírse de to laugh at

relajarse to relax

relatar to report

renovar to renew

reñir to quarrel

reparar to repair, to mend

repartir to deal; to deliver

repetir(se) to repeat

reponer to replace
  reponerse to mend

representar to perform; to represent
requerir to require
resbalar to slide
reservar to book; to reserve
resistir to hold out
  resistir(se) to resist
resolver to solve
respetar to respect
respirar to breathe
responder to reply, to answer;
  to respond
restaurar to restore
resultar to prove
retar to challenge
retirar(se) to withdraw
reunir(se) to collect
  reunirse to gather; **reunirse con**
  to rejoin
revelar to reveal
rodear (de) to surround (with)
romper(se) to break; to tear;
  to burst
ruborizarse to blush
saber a to taste of
saber to know
  sé nadar I can swim
sacar to bring out; to take out
  sacar brillo to polish; **sacarse el**
  título to qualify
sacudir to shake
salir to emerge
saltar to leap
saludar to greet
  saludar con la cabeza to nod
salvar to rescue; to save
secar(se) to dry
seguir to follow
  seguir haciendo algo to go on
  doing sth

sentarse to sit (down)
sentir to be sorry
  sentir(se) to feel
señalizar to indicate
ser to be
servir to serve
significar to mean
sobrevivir to survive
solicitar to apply to; to seek
soltar to release
sonar to sound
  (hacer) sonar to ring
sonreír to smile
sorprender to surprise
sospechar to suspect
subir to climb; to come up; to go up
  subir a to board; to get on
suceder to happen
sufrir (de) to suffer (from)
  sufrir un colapso to collapse
sugerir to suggest
sujetar to fix
suministrar to supply
suponer to assume; to suppose;
  to involve
surgir to emerge
suspender to suspend; to fail
suspirar to sigh
sustituir to replace
telefonear to telephone
temblar to shake
temer to fear
tender to hold out
tener to have; to hold
  tener antipatía a to dislike; **tener**
  cuidado to be careful; **tener éxito**
  to be successful; **tener lugar**
  to take place; to come off; **tener**
  mala suerte to be unlucky; **tener**

miedo to be afraid; **tener que** to have to; **tener que ver con** to concern; **tener razón** to be right; **tener suerte** to be lucky; **tener tendencia a hacer algo** to tend to do sth
terminar to end; to finish
tirar to throw away
  tirar de to pull
tocar to touch; to play; to ring
tomar to take
torcer to twist
trabajar to work
traducir to translate
traer to bring
traicionar to betray
tranquilizar(se) to calm down
trasladar to transfer
tratar to treat
  tratar (de) to try (to); **tratar con** to deal with
unir to join
  unir(se) to unite

untar to spread
usar to use
vaciar(se) to empty
vacilar to hesitate
valer to be worth
variar to vary
vencer to conquer, to defeat, to overcome
vender to stock
  vender(se) to sell
venir to come
  venirse abajo to collapse
ver to see
visitar to visit
vislumbrar to catch sight of
vivir to live
volar to fly
volcar to overturn
volver to come back; to go back; to return
  volver(se) to turn round; **volverse hacia** to turn towards
votar to vote

ENGLISH
INDEX

The words on the following pages cover all of the ESSENTIAL
and IMPORTANT NOUNS in the book.